Sunday Adelaja is a leading figure not only in Ukraine but also in the world. He has a spirit of faith driven by his compassion for people. The word he speaks is one of authority!

—BILLY JOE DAUGHERTY
VICTORY CHRISTIAN CENTER
TULSA, OK

Some are called to churches. Some are called to cities. Sunday Adelaja has a fresh word for the nations! His experience with the Lord, his compassion for people, and his commitment to the kingdom make Sunday Adelaja a world-class leader with a world-class vision to build a world-class army to change the world for Christ. This world-class book is a must for you today. Read and reap benefits for a lifetime.

—KENNETH C. ULMER, DMIN, PHD
PRESIDING BISHOP
MACEDONIA INTERNATIONAL BIBLE FELLOWSHIP

Sunday Adelaja is an indisputable success in his family, in his church, in his nation. This book will help you grow personally and spiritually. Read it and SUCCEED!

—PETER LOWE
FOUNDER AND CEO
GET MOTIVATED SEMINARS

Several years ago I was discarding items from an overgrown stack of mail. One brochure caught my eye. As I read, I was gripped by Sunday Adelaja's brilliant grasp of the interrelationship between biblical truths and public policy. Instead of trashing it, I showed the article to others. If one brochure is that enlightening, think what an entire book might be.

—Dr. Jim Garlow
Senior Pastor, Skyline Wesleyan Church
San Diego, CA

I have heard and read a great deal about Pastor Sunday and about the work he is doing. All those who do great things go through attacks such as Pastor Sunday has endured.

—U.S. President Bill Clinton

I know of no minister around the world who is more unique and influential than Bishop Sunday Adelaja. I count him as a wonderful friend in the kingdom and pray God's divine protection and direction over his dynamic ministry. The supernatural principles of this book are radical, controversial, and life changing. They will make ministers of the gospel reconsider their place and calling in ministry. Our minds will be stretched and our concepts will be challenged, as they should be, for more effective twenty-first-century ministry and preparation for the coming of the Lord.

—Dr. Wendell Smith
The City Church
Seattle, WA

Strong kingdom visionary leadership is required in order to fulfill the Great Commission in our lifetime. Pastor Sunday Adelaja presents a powerful pathway to empower both the pastor and the church for societal transformation.

—Phil Pringle
Christian City Churches
Sydney, Australia

In order to reclaim America's communities, a dynamic leadership paradigm shift will need to take place in our local churches. Pastor

Sunday Adelaja has provided a pathway for us to achieve success in the years ahead. Read it and reap from it!

—Alton Garrison
Assistant General Superintendent
Assemblies of God
Springfield, Missouri

The most successful in contemporary European churches is the Ukraine-based ministry of Sunday Adelaja.

—Philip Jenkins
Distinguished Professor of History and Religious Studies
Pennsylvania State University
Missiologist, Author of *The Next Christendom: The Coming of Global Christianity*

Sunday Adelaja brings to you one of the greatest Christian hero stories of the modern world. Reading these pages, you will be inspired to live a greater life than you have ever dreamed possible. Your fear will be turned into faith, your burdens into blessings, and your impossibilities into possibilities in Christ. Think of Pastor Sunday in terms of: "These that have turned the world upside down are come hither also" (Acts 17:6, kjv).

—James O. Davis
Co-Chair/Founder Second Billion

Pastor Sunday Adelaja has been mightily used by the Lord to transform his society for Christ. In his book *ChurchShift*, he teaches how one can learn how to take full responsibility and begin to climb the ladder of true greatness in life. If you desire to live at the highest possible leadership level, then this book is a must for you.

—Pastor Stan Toler
Trinity Church of the Nazarene
Oklahoma City, OK

ChurchShift is a study on the contemporary application of the relevant kingdom principles taught by Jesus Christ and gives evidence that the real mission, purpose, and mandate of the church is not to abandon the earth but to affect and infect it with the culture and nature of heaven. I recommend this book to all and believe it will become a classic.

—Dr. Myles E. Munroe
Founder/President, BFM International
International Third World Leaders Association
(ITWLA)

Thank you for your contribution to our common victory. Your conscious work is a considerable factor in that victory. It was you who protected democracy in Ukraine, standing for its high ideals and not considering your own interests. I am convinced that as long as there are people in Ukraine who have the same civil position, dignity, and spirit as you have, everything will be all right in this country.

—Victor Yushchenko
President of Ukraine

Through Pastor Sunday's endeavors, we have become bold and fearless people who are able to stand for truth, liberty, and God.

—Leonid Chernovetskiy
Mayor of Kyiv

ChurchShift will stretch your mind through God-given principles being applied in personal and powerful ways. You will understand your uniqueness in Christ and will have greater faith to experience supernatural results.

—David Mohan
Founding Pastor, New Life Assembly
Chennai, India

Just as Moses was a meek leader who impacted change in a nation by the power of God, so has Sunday Adelaja. In a meek yet bold way, Pastor Sunday shows the world how to make the gospel socially relevant. His words will challenge you. His story will inspire you!

—BISHOP DALE C. BRONNER, DMIN
WORD OF FAITH FAMILY WORSHIP CATHEDRAL
ATLANTA, GA

The Great Commission includes saving souls and planting churches, but it is much more than just that. God's mandate to us is nothing less than taking dominion of His entire creation here on Earth. No one has put this mandate into practice more wisely and effectively than my good friend Sunday Adelaja. Of all the excellent new books on aggressively advancing the kingdom of God, this one stands out as being the most practical.

—C. PETER WAGNER
PRESIDING APOSTLE
INTERNATIONAL COALITION OF APOSTLES

Sunday has practically applied the principles of the kingdom to his life, church, city, nation, and the world in every sphere of life, and it is bringing transformation. The only hope of seeing transformation in our world is the living out of the principles he teaches from God's Word about the kingdom. Rock on, Sunday! Read this book—then apply it.

—BOB ROBERTS
PASTOR, NORTHWOOD CHURCH
KELLER, TX
AUTHOR, *TRANSFORMATION* AND *GLOCALIZATION*

Pastor Sunday is a young old man: young because of his age of less than forty years old, and old because at such a young age he has known what old men like me know and has been able to accomplish what many old men like me have not been able to accomplish.

—T. L. OSBORN
INTERNATIONAL EVANGELIST
TULSA, OK

Sunday Adelaja and I share a hero—Dr. D. James Kennedy. Through Dr. Kennedy's passion for both the evangelism mandate and the cultural mandate, Pastor Sunday was inspired to equip his congregation to impact public life. What a mark Pastor Sunday has made on Ukraine, Europe, and the world! I applaud his vision for ministry.

—John Sorensen
Executive Vice President
Evangelism Explosion International

This book will be a catalyst in leading a strategic church in today's world. When you read about the awesome experiences of Pastor Sunday, it will inspire you to believe God for "greater things." I cannot wait to see this book published and read by thousands of pastors and church leaders like me who are hungry for a powerful and extraordinary move of God to impact our cities and nations.

—David A. Sobrepeña
Founding Pastor, Word of Hope Church
Manila, Philippines

Favor may open doors, but influence changes nations. Sunday Adelaja is a man of great influence for the cause of Christ. His anointing services in Kyiv in a massive sports stadium are so dynamic, diverse, and exciting that when they end after five hours, no one wants to leave! Simply spectacular! That is the man Sunday Adelaja—simple truth, spectacular faith, massive results. Catch the largeness of his spirit, and find the greatness of God unfolding in your life.

—Paul Louis Cole
President, Christian Men's Network

In today's fatherless world, where men abdicate their roles and shun responsibility, God must raise up fathers who will accept responsibility for families, communities, and nations. Sunday Adelaja, a fatherless child, has become a father to a nation. This book reveals the Father's heart and inspires us to act on what is right.

—J. Doug Stringer
Founder and President, Somebody Cares
Houston, TX

In *ChurchShift*, Sunday Adelaja articulates the greatest need Christians have today—for churches not just to be large in influence. This book will help not only to build churches but also to take nations.

—Alexey Ledyaev
Senior Pastor, New Generation Churches
Riga, Latvia

Kingdom leaders expand our spiritual horizons and cause us to see the world from God's perspective. Pastor Sunday Adelaja's classic book *ChurchShift* challenges the reader to trust God for the resources required in order to bring societal transformation. In your quest for maximum spiritual growth, this invaluable book will change your life forever. Read it now and reap a lifetime.

—J. Don George
Pastor, Calvary Church
Irving, TX

The words in this book come from a man who is a living testimony. If you want transformation and not just information, then you need to read words from someone who has been transformed. Pastor Sunday's revolutionary message is well described in these pages. This book provides God's model for transformation and the mind-set of a Christ-centered revolution, all from an incredible man who has led and experienced them both.

—Dr. Ben Lerner
New York Times Best-selling Author
U.S. Olympic Team Physician

Sunday Adelaja is one of those new breed of men who is influencing a nation and modeling a new style of missions. While there are some men who see success in another church or nation and follow their example, Pastor Sunday is that example that men from around the world hear about and follow. He is a cross-cultural missionary who has made a new mold of what missions can do to touch a nation. I consider Pastor Sunday a modern-day hero of the faith.

—Pastor Robert Barriger
Camino de Vida
Lima, Peru

Sunday Adelaja's ministry inspires people all over the world. For those who live where Christians are persecuted, we are encouraged to see God quickly bring a nation from religious repression to freedom of religion and democracy. We are inspired to see God use a pastor to bring national transformation. Thank you, Sunday, for providing hope and for setting such a bold example.

—Eddy Leo
Pastor, Abbalove Ministries
Jakarta, Indonesia

If there is one book that can change your life, you're holding it in your hand. *ChurchShift* is one of the most important and timely messages that you will ever read. It's revolutionary. I encourage every minister to study this book.

—Sam Hinn
Senior Pastor, The Gathering Place Worship Center
Sanford, FL

The Embassy of God church is the biggest church in Ukraine and well organized with different areas and ministries. Pastor Sunday is a unique man. It makes no difference that he is black or that he is

Nigerian or that he is not from Ukraine. This is a big church that keeps growing every day.

—Vasiliy Onopenko
Chairman of the Supreme Court of Ukraine

God has raised up Sunday Adelaja to lead men and women to a deeper understanding of their spiritual destinies. Read this book, and let the journey begin.

—Rear Admiral Barry Black (Ret.)
Chaplain, U.S. Senate

Nothing like the Embassy of God has ever been seen before in Ukraine.

—British Broadcasting Corporation (BBC)

The Embassy of The Blessed Kingdom of God for All Nations church has ballooned from a ministry for society's troubled into this ex-Soviet republic's first true megachurch.

—Associated Press (AP)

Pastor Sunday is a man with a mission.

—*Wall Street Journal*

CHURCH
SHIFT

SUNDAY ADELAJA

Charisma
HOUSE
A STRANG COMPANY

Most Strang Communications/Charisma House/Christian Life/Siloam/Excel Books/FrontLine/Realms products are available at special quantity discounts for bulk purchase for sales promotions, premiums, fund-raising, and educational needs. For details, write Strang Communications/Charisma House/Christian Life/Siloam/Excel Books/FrontLine/Realms, 600 Rinehart Road, Lake Mary, Florida 32746, or telephone (407) 333-0600.

ChurchShift by Sunday Adelaja
Published by Charisma House
A Strang Company
600 Rinehart Road
Lake Mary, Florida 32746
www.strangdirect.com

Cover Designer: studiogearbox.com
Executive Design Director: Bill Johnson

Library of Congress Cataloging-in-Publication Data

Adelaja, Sunday.
  Church shift / Sunday Adelaja. -- 1st ed.
    p. cm.
  ISBN 978-1-59979-097-8 (trade paper)
  1. Christian life. I. Title.

  BV4501.3.A335 2007
  248.4--dc22

                                    2007016720

International Standard Book Number: 978-1-59979-097-8

First Edition

08 09 10 11 12 — 11 10 9 8 7 6 5 4
Printed in the United States of America

For my grandmother, Mrs. Rachel Adelaja (Nee Awolana), who picked me up when my mother and father had forsaken me, and trained me into a man of virtue.

Acknowledgments

I WOULD LIKE TO THANK BOSE ADELAJA, MY WIFE. Thank you for being my support and encourager and understanding my numerous travels overseas and all the time I needed to spend alone with God. I would like to thank Perez, Zoe, and Pearl—my children—for their time in letting Daddy go to work on this book and when I am called away for ministry. Thank you, Stephen Strang, and your team, who worked to get this message published and Barbara Dycus and Joel Kilpatrick, who edited the book. I would like to acknowledge my friend James O. Davis, the founder of the Second Billion movement, and Joann Webster for all the advice and support you have given me.

Contents

A WORD FROM THE AUTHOR

I n November 2006, I wedged myself between the armrests of an airline seat and settled in for the long flight back to Kyiv from one of my numerous trips overseas. Without much room to maneuver, I just leaned my head back to pray. My prayers soon turned into meditations about where I'd just been, where I was going, and the overall state of the church worldwide. Suddenly, an image of the globe came to my mind. I could sense the burden God has for His church to be reformed in order to be capable of gathering in the last harvest.

From that vision, I came to understand that God is not satisfied with the state of the modern church. Most leaders I've met worldwide would agree that we collectively have a great deal of work left to do, regardless of the great strides we have made. With five billion people still unsaved, we must gain ground. What struck me is that if we are to see Jesus come back any time soon, the church must be reformed once again. What humbled me, though, was the impression that God was challenging me to do something about it. This was in direct conflict with where I was in my comfort zone of ministry at that time.

The challenge to play a role in the restoration of the church reminded me of a time of prayer I had in spring of 2004. At that time, God challenged me to take responsibility for Ukraine. That experience led to the events of the Orange Revolution in Ukraine, which I thought was the ultimate. Now I was sensing that the victories in Ukraine had only been a preparation for this new challenge.

As I prayed about the vision over the next few months, I received clear direction on my role in this latest reformation. My first duty that became abundantly clear was that I should write a book that addresses areas where the church must have a shift to leave the old and bring in the new. The result is what you are holding in your hand now: *ChurchShift*.

May the Lord God of heaven use this humble work to help touch and transform His church. I pray that the little lessons I've been taught behind the iron curtain of communism will be a blessing to the wider body of Christ.

It was the missionaries and their supporters, Bible providers, intercessors, charity workers, smugglers, and martyrs sent by the West who reached my family for Christ, provided water to my village in Nigeria, then gave me materials and needed support while I struggled in my Christian walk behind the iron curtain. It is God's perfect plan of sowing and reaping that He would now send me to return the benefits of all He taught me while under their care.

My prayer is that every church leader, pastor, or bishop will read this book and use its workbook to make a study in home groups, cells, small groups, home churches, Sunday schools, and Bible colleges. May the lessons inside this book not be lost but bring us all to shift to help gather in the last harvest.

Let the revolution begin!

—**Pastor Sunday**

Prologue

Y ADOPTED HOME COUNTRY OF UKRAINE became the center of world attention in the fall of 2004. In one of the most joyous and peaceful revolutions the world has ever seen, the people cast off the yoke of political oppression that had rested on our necks ever since the Soviet Union made Ukraine a vassal state half a century earlier. Though communism was gone now, a Moscow-backed hard-line government was trying to steal Ukraine's presidential election and keep the country under the thumb of Russia. The democratic process was being subverted by leaders who had no respect for liberty or the rule of law. The people of Ukraine were headed again toward servitude.

But this time was different. This time the people of Ukraine rose up and said, "Enough!" Not only that, but also God put the church I pastor, the Embassy of the Blessed Kingdom of God for All Nations, on the front lines of an amazing national transformation.

Our church played a leading role in toppling the corrupt powers and ushering in a new era of freedom for our country.

People are amazed to hear that there is a megachurch like ours in such a dark place as Europe. With twenty-five thousand members, the Embassy of God is one of the largest churches on the European continent and in the world. People did not think such a thing was possible, but God has done it. The church and I have been the subject of much media attention, including a front-page article in the *Wall Street Journal* and profiles in the *Washington Post*, the BBC, and much more. But people are even more surprised to hear that I, a native Nigerian, pastor this church, which is 99.9 percent white. They wonder how a black man like me ended up in Ukraine and why I was ever accepted as a spiritual leader. But God has placed me here to do something unique and revolutionary. He plucked me from my small village in Africa, where I was motherless, fatherless, and so poor that I could barely afford shoes until I was twelve, and He educated me under a communist state during the cold war. Then He brought me by divine call to Ukraine and told me to start a church in Kyiv (pronounced "keev") in 1994. Since then God has done much more than anyone could have expected. He has brought a shift in our individual lives, in our city, and in our nation. These principles, I believe, are to be embraced by people everywhere—including you.

The revolution in Ukraine did not begin in the halls of power or political backrooms. It began in the prayer closet. It began when our church discovered how to shift society as individuals and as a body of believers. As I looked out on the vast crowds that filled Independence Square during the revolution, I knew that God used our church as a spiritual icebreaker six months earlier when we had held an unprecedented protest at this very spot. Under God's direction, we had been used to change the mind-set of an entire country.

Hope had risen in a proud nation that for too long had been ruled by unjust slave masters. I believe that the protest and prayers by our church and other churches led to the most important change in Ukraine in centuries.

It was a dramatic demonstration that God intends for all believers to occupy their personal promised land and that our combined efforts to follow kingdom principles can transform entire nations.

That is the message of this book. God has a plan to help you find your promised land and teach you how to fully occupy it. God's intention is to transform your life, your promised land, and your nation and to use you to bring back the earth to Himself, just as He is doing with us in Ukraine. As believers, our first calling is to be part of this master plan. National transformation is at the heart of the Great Commission. It is the primary calling of everyone who follows Christ. This book will redefine your life by redefining what the Great Commission means for you. You will see your earthly assignment in a new way and receive the tools and strategies to carry out your calling with greater effectiveness than ever before. The principles you learn in these pages will help you to establish the kingdom of God in your everyday life and in your nation by applying kingdom principles that dethrone the kingdom of darkness.

Best of all, this book is based on real experiences, not theories. This is not my wishful thinking but rather present-day reality. I believe God chose to demonstrate these kingdom principles in spiritually desolate Europe to prove that any person can find his or her promised land and impact the people and society where God has placed him or her.

I now bring those principles to you. You too can find your promised land and bring the kingdom of God right where you live, work, and play. You too can transform your nation for Christ by taking simple steps in your everyday life to establish His rule and invite His glory.

One day the church and its people worldwide will no longer be humiliated and downtrodden but will lead nations. We will be the head, not the tail. We will pioneer social answers instead of always playing catch-up. I pray this book and its message will usher in a revolution in your life and your nation that is bigger than any revolution the world has yet seen.

Brother, sister, get ready to shift!

Chapter 1

PEOPLE POWER

—————

I COULD NOT BELIEVE WHAT GOD WAS TELLING ME TO do. I kept pacing the floor in my place of prayer where I had determined to spend a week alone with God. And I kept resisting Him.

"But Lord, what you're telling me to do is unsanctioned and dangerous," I said. "We could be shot. The government might bring their tanks out. People might be killed. At the very least our reputation in Ukraine could be ruined."

But God was not budging. During that entire week I spent in prayer, His answer to me remained the same: He wanted my church to openly protest against our government in Kyiv.

In my mind this was not just foolish, it was dangerous. It was like declaring war on the government. We could be treated harshly, jailed, or shot, as had happened to protesters in the past.

Even though Ukraine was not officially communist anymore, the people of the nation still lived under a mind-set of oppression. For many years the Soviet Union had taught the Ukrainian people to unquestionably submit to authority. Though the Soviet Union was gone, people still couldn't imagine a government that respected them. So the government felt free to treat people as sheep and servants. There was no accountability in the leadership as there is in a democracy. Leaders were as corrupt as they wanted to be, and the people simply accepted it as the way things would always be. They continued to hide their thoughts and feelings deep down inside and pretended to agree with the government. Even though Ukraine had become independent more than a decade earlier, people still feared that the persecutions and concentration camps of the Soviet era would somehow return.

As a result there were no protests and few peaceful gatherings in Ukraine. People did not want to provoke the government. They were fatalistic. The country was frozen in place. Nobody dared step out of line. The underlying threat of violence or hardship against anyone who promoted what the government deemed "social upheaval" was well understood. Groups that gathered without government approval could be met with bullets and tanks, prison terms, harassment, or at least the scorn of the country. It was one thing for a political group to protest, but it was an entirely different thing for a church to bring out its people in a mass protest.

For us, a church already viewed with suspicion by many Ukrainians, any hint of civil disobedience was very risky. Pastoring an evangelical church in Ukraine and other Eastern European countries is a delicate tightrope walk between a hostile culture, suspicious government leaders, a highly educated atheist elite, and unjust laws that keep your church disenfranchised. Ukraine prizes itself on its educational system, all atheist based, that has produced fourteen Nobel Prize winners. As the motherland of the Orthodox church, Ukraine people are conditioned to believe that the Orthodox church is the only true church, an emblem of their culture more than a place to worship God, and that other churches are cults, foreign interlopers, even cover organizations for spies. We had fought that impression for years by working peacefully in Ukraine and serving the people. We started a soup kitchen that fed two thousand people daily—more than a million people overall. We raised up businessmen in the church through our business training programs. We held marriage preparation courses, counseling for unwed mothers, and men's conferences that helped to create strong families and a more stable society. We worked in AIDS prevention and drug rehabilitation, helping three thousand people to become free from addictions. We were curing many of society's ills without a penny of government money. We were doing the work of God without posing a threat to anyone. We were serving Ukraine in love.

But our country still treated us with suspicion and made laws to constrain us. In fact, we were facing a crisis at that moment because as a "cult" we were told we were not allowed to buy land, even though ours was the largest evangelical church in all of Europe. Imagine having a church of thousands and being barred from building your own sanctuary. That was our situation (and it continues to be the situation for many or most evangelical churches in the former Soviet Union). The Orthodox church and its allies in the government had painted us as an army of zombies and accused me of being a charismatic leader who kept the church members hypnotized. Never mind that the Embassy of God fed more people than the city government of Kyiv and that all our efforts were making the country more stable and prosperous. We were still labeled a threat to Ukraine's national identity.

We had avoided direct confrontation with the government for a decade, but then our building lease came up for renewal, and the government decided to kick us out so they could renovate the property. We had nowhere else to go. No place was large enough. Bulldozers were parked outside our current facility, waiting to move in. Soon we were forced to meet outside in the rain and snow for our services. The largest church in Europe had become homeless.

At the beginning of the crisis I had done what I always did— I went to God. He had never failed me, and I knew He would have our solution. I wasn't the least bit worried, but as I prayed, I received no answer. God seemed silent. I prayed for months, then for a full year, as the tractors moved in and our lease expired and the building's owners shut off the plumbing. Our people began to wonder where we would go. Still, God gave me no guidance on the subject. His silence shook me more than anything. I could handle government oppression— I had been dealing with that since I had come to the Soviet Union in the 1980s. I could handle crises involving our church location. We had moved often, changing locations half a dozen times in one five-year period. We had bounced all around the city—and still had grown. Man-made problems didn't alarm me. But the silence of God did. Where was my ever-present help? What had I done wrong?

Finally, His reply came during a time of intense prayer: "Stand up to the city government. Don't let them shove you around anymore." His answer challenged me to my core. I was so unprepared to accept it that I cleared my schedule and took another week in prayer to make sure I had heard correctly. I prayed all day for seven days, and God's message to me did not change. He was preparing us to have a bigger impact than I had anticipated. We just had to learn to listen.

PEOPLE POWER

God told me to take our church to the streets of Kyiv in protest. "The people are the power," He said. "Use the power you have." Such a move was unprecedented in Ukraine. But God opened my eyes to see that to complete the Great Commission, we must have impact upon nations, not just people in churches. Transforming nations requires bold steps. We could no longer be concerned with just preserving what we had or adding numbers to our congregation; we were being called to move strongly into every sphere of society. That included using methods we had never considered, like public protest.

My views on civil disobedience were traditional and conservative. I believed Christians were never to disobey or demonstrate against the government but rather to humbly submit to it because it bears God's authority and power to punish. I was not afraid of the punishment, but I certainly wanted to obey God, and so I taught myself and my people to honor the government and comply with its laws.

But in that place of prayer, alone and broken, God showed me I was wrong. He took me through the Book of Acts and showed me that civil disobedience can be righteous when you are fighting unrighteousness. He showed me how the disciples had disobeyed the law when the law prohibited them from preaching in the name of Jesus. (See Acts 5.) I had never seen that as civil disobedience before, but now I did. Not only did they disobey the law, but also God backed them up in it. In our situation, even though peaceful demonstrations were allowed by law, we still needed special permission from the government to conduct such a protest. Those special permissions were never issued.

I left that time of prayer sure of what I needed to do. God's message rang in my ears: "The people are the power. Use the people."

I announced to our church leaders what we had to do, and many of them rejected it out of hand.

"That's suicide," said one.

"It's unbiblical," said a few others.

I had already girded myself, knowing I would have to do battle with my friends before fighting the real battle in the streets of Kyiv. Then I told the church what I believed God wanted us do. Letters of resignation arrived on my desk almost immediately. "We have families and businesses," people wrote. "We are afraid. We don't want the government to clamp down on us like in communist times."

To try to restore unity, I told the church leadership to take a week off and seek God for an answer. These twelve men did that, and they came back with a confirmation of what God had told me. They were as astonished as I had been, and now they too were preparing for the battle to come. God was about to teach us one of the most important lessons to influence a nation, which is: you will never accomplish it if you remain within the four walls of the church.

Through it all we were discovering what the Great Commission really means. God had been teaching us that our mission as believers is to save nations, not just evangelize individuals and build churches. God is not terribly concerned with church size and church ministries. These are all sidelights to His main goal, which is for all nations to walk after Him in kingdom principles. The church fulfills its mandate when it changes society, not when it's confined to its sanctuary and Sunday school classrooms. The church is to build the kingdom of God in a nation. The kingdom must overflow into streets and workplaces, governments and entertainment venues. That is its nature, to grow and take over. If you try to keep it to yourself, you lose it.

And we didn't want to lose it.

CHURCH-FOCUSED CHURCHES

Too many Christians and Christian leaders spend their energy, creativity, and precious time promoting churches instead of the kingdom. They work for the success of their church, or perhaps for a group of churches in their city, or they work for their ministry or denomination. They believe that by building churches and ministries they are building the kingdom. They think *church* and *kingdom* are practically synonymous. This isolation of the church from the world has led to ineffectiveness and failure to carry out the Great Commission.

But the church is not the kingdom. Jesus said in Luke 17:21, "Nor will people say, 'Here it is,' or 'There it is,' because the kingdom of God is within you." It's not confined to temples and churches. No church can contain or control the kingdom of God. The kingdom is meant to inhabit the entire earth, not just your church sanctuary.

The Great Commission is not what many of us have understood it to be. We have understood it to be evangelism—bringing people from the world into our church buildings. But the Great Commission mandate is to go out and disciple nations. The focus is not *in here*, but *out there*. This was Jesus's goal in coming to Earth. It is supposed to be our goal as redeemed people. The Great Commission in Matthew 28:19 says:

Go and make disciples of all nations.

Jesus did not say, "Go and build great churches." He did not even say, "Go and save individuals." He never said, "May thy church come on Earth as it is in heaven." Neither did He say, "Seek ye first the church and all its righteousness." Rather, His heartbeat is for nations to be ruled by kingdom principles. That is the calling of every believer and of every church.

So why has our attention been lavished on personal evangelism and building churches? The problem is our mind-set. We often forget that the kingdom has come. We forget we have been called to rule our promised lands—and to rule nations. We forget about the power we received from Jesus Christ. So our attention is drawn to churches. Building a church seems much more manageable than transforming a nation.

My own religious background taught me that the kingdom of God was all about heaven, not Earth. I thought kingdom work took place after we die, once we had passed over into the kingdom. I misread the Bible and the words of Jesus. I made the kingdom of God all about the future, and so my focus and purpose in life were off course. I was having little impact on the world around me. But because God wanted to do something in Ukraine that was much bigger than our "big church" or me, He graciously taught us to take a proactive position in society, to go outside our building and enforce His authority over an ungodly nation and government.

Today many people sit in church pews hoping to make it to the kingdom of God, and they don't realize that, according to Jesus, the kingdom is here and now. Nobody has to die to see the kingdom. We are as close as we will ever get. Jesus didn't leave the kingdom of God in heaven when He came to Earth. He brought it with Him. The born-again believer is in the kingdom at this moment. We can stop hoping for it—it came two thousand years ago, and it is present with us now.

When we forget that the kingdom is here and now, we shrink from our calling to disciple nations. We want to use the church as our escape hatch from the world's problems. The battle is certainly fierce, but God is sending Christians not to hide out in, or even build, churches but to have impact in their lives and on the nations of the world. If you are trying only to build a church, your goal is wrong. The promise of God is, "Ask of me, and I will make the nations your inheritance" (Ps. 2:8).

Imagine that! We are meant to inherit nations. We are responsible not for sanctuaries and Sunday school rooms but for our nations. We are not separate from our nations in God's sight. We belong to nations. God will hold us responsible for nations. We cannot flee into the church and think our hands will be washed clean of all that happens outside. We are called to the world to restore the kingdom. And if there is any nation that is suffering under a godless culture, it's because Christians have not subdued it with kingdom principles. God did not answer our church's many prayers to resolve our problem of having a place of worship because He had something bigger in mind—the salvation of the nation, not just providing a new place for us to gather.

Some people believe that if they work in the nursery or sing in the choir, they are fulfilling their area of ministry. But this is not really ministry. It is merely housekeeping. Your work as a choir member, nursery volunteer, or usher is what we all must do to keep the church functioning, but it is not necessarily fulfilling the Great Commission. The Great Commission happens outside the church. Ministry is what you do to bring your life and your sphere of influence under kingdom rule.

THE KINGDOM-DRIVEN CHURCH

Church has never been the focus of the Great Commission, but it has always been the most important tool for carrying out the Great Commission. The church is the primary vehicle God uses to train people so they know how to find their promised land and rule in their nation. Church is the headquarters, but battles are not fought at headquarters. They are fought in the field.

First Timothy 3:15 calls the church the pillar and foundation of the truth. It upholds the kingdom by being the school, the equipping place, and the place of support for world changers. But our focus must remain outside, not inside. We are to go from the "school" into the world and bring the powerful kingdom principles to bear on its problems.

When Christians change the goal of the church and make it a place of conservation and escape rather than equipping and sending, we are working against the Great Commission. We are conserving crowds, not sending them out. We are hoarding kingdom resources, namely, people and their gifts. In many churches, God's workers are in captivity. They are like prisoners and the pastors are the wardens.

We are not called to huddle inside the church sanctuary but to restore the kingdom of God to the world. But some Christians and preachers misinterpret the word *ecclesia*, the Greek word for "church," which means literally "called-out ones." They mistakenly believe it means we are to be "called away from the world." This is a grave error. Jesus said in John 17:15, "My prayer is not that you take them out of the world but that you protect them from the evil one."

As a church we are "called out" from the evil principles of this world, but we are still required to live here. We are not built for monasteries. Our calling is to operate from a different and superior set of principles than the world we live in. The church is to train us to be Christlike, to embody Jesus and His principles, so that in everyday life we may operate from a godly perspective. That's what the church is for. That's why we come on Sunday. That's why we preach, teach, and worship together.

God holds the church responsible for societies. It is the most potent organization in the world because it was started by Jesus and is His bride. No other entity in the world is as important as the church, in spite of all its failures; it is the hope of God because through it, and only it, the kingdom can come.

But the church is only relevant on Earth. It is irrelevant in heaven. When the church gets to heaven, it will become one with Christ. So the task of the church is here and now to bring the kingdom to Earth. Churches come and go, but the kingdom is everlasting.

Our focus must be on the kingdom and on redeeming nations. The church is to be the training ground for people who will impact the society around them.

As I and the people in my church began to grasp our kingdom calling, our fear melted away. We decided to take the massive risk and march on city hall, even in the face of danger. "The people are the power," God had told me. It was time to take that power to the streets. Little did we know that this act of obedience to a divine instruction from heaven, though unconventional, would go a long way to shaping the history of our nation.

As we obeyed, we learned impacting principles that we had never discovered before. I will share them with you now. It's what I call "churchshift."

KINGDOM PRINCIPLES
FROM CHAPTER 1

1. The church fulfills its mandate when it changes society, not when it is confined to its sanctuary and Sunday school classrooms.

2. This isolation of the church from the world has led to ineffectiveness and failure to carry out the Great Commission.

3. The Great Commission mandate is to go out and disciple nations.

4. Ministry is what you do to bring your life and your sphere of influence under kingdom rule.

5. We are not called to huddle inside the church sanctuary but to restore the kingdom of God to the world.

6. God holds the church responsible for societies.

7. The church is to be the training ground for people who will impact the society around them.

Chapter 2

THE KINGDOM-
MINDED CHURCH

T HE DECISION TO STAND UP TO OUR GOVERNMENT was not our first effort to reach our nation for God, but it was the most dramatic to date, and it became a watershed moment for us and for the entire nation of Ukraine. We had very good reason to believe our lives were in danger. The last time any group had gone to the streets in such massive protest was a few years before, and people had been shot. So we proceeded very carefully. We requested permission from the city to gather. The city denied us permission. We tried every angle we could to conform to the law, but we were stonewalled.

Opposition from within the church also increased. More people wrote letters of resignation. Others loudly opposed our plans. They wanted to remain at the level of safety and influence we'd always had. But God had spoken: if we did not move forward down this difficult avenue, the kingdom would stop advancing through us. We could not let that happen.

On Monday, November 13, 2003, three thousand members of our church took the bravest step of our lives and marched on city hall. We took buses to the city center and walked a kilometer to city hall. As we flooded the streets, traffic stopped. Commerce all but halted. Nothing could move.

There was an unexpected surprise: the prime minister of Turkey was visiting that day, and the country's capital was paralyzed—by a church group! We were rejoicing, blessing everyone in sight, carrying big banners, celebrating, and singing praises. The government was embarrassed to have this incident during a state visit and wanted to avoid national disgrace.

We arrived at city hall and held an outdoor meeting. We prayed for the government, then spoke to the leaders through a megaphone: "We elected you. You are supposed to serve us, so we are blessing you, praying for you. Don't be against your own people."

I appealed to them to extend the lease on our land or provide us land to build on. But the city hall building remained quiet. Nobody came out. In an atmosphere of growing tension, we wondered what their response would be.

DOES GOD REALLY CARE ABOUT NATIONS?

Many people in today's church have a hard time believing that God cares about nations and societies. They think He is solely concerned with individuals or with His chosen people. But the Bible is very clear: God wants to redeem nations. His redemptive work on the cross is for nations as well as individuals. That's why He said to go preach the gospel to all nations and to disciple nations. God eagerly awaits the redemption of the nations.

Throughout the Bible, God's nation focus is clear. In a significant passage in Exodus 4:22, God uses interesting language to describe the nation of Israel. He calls it, "My son, My firstborn" (NKJV). It is instructive that God uses a first-person description for a nation. Normally, *son* refers to an individual. In Malachi 3:17 God did it again, speaking through the prophet that He would spare Israel "as a man spares his own son who serves him" (NKJV). I believe God is teaching us about His attitude toward nations. In His eyes, nations are not just some abstract entity. Nations are as tangible and precious to Him as individuals.

If God saved the nation of Israel, His firstborn, logically He wants to do the same for all other nations, which are His children. Israel was the beginning of a global campaign. God wants preeminence in all things in every nation. Jesus promised in Matthew 24:14, "And this gospel of the kingdom will be preached in the whole world as a testimony to all nations, and then the end will come." He wants to adopt as sons all nations, not just individuals. In Matthew 28:18–20, He gave "all authority in heaven and on earth" to the disciples to be used to disciple nations, not just individuals. There will be no end to the increase of His government, says Isaiah 9:7.

Have you ever wondered why God has such great respect for man's governments? Why does He teach us to obey and respect them and submit to their authority? If God is only concerned with saving individuals, why doesn't He tell us to simply ignore man's systems of rule? The reason is that government is God's idea. He has a government of His own, and He wants men to rule justly on the earth in their own governments. God created governments as systems of justice for Himself. He wants to administer the earth with justice through kingdom-minded leaders. Even if the government is being administered badly, it is still a God-ordained institution. That's why Paul said in Romans that every government is from God. As kingdom people we are not allowed to ignore governments, because they are established by God and are part of His plan for this earth. Our purpose is to make those governments act justly and according to all kingdom principles.

Church reformers like Martin Luther in previous ages had this national focus; they wanted to bring nations to their knees before God. But today too many Christians have scaled back their ambitions. It's time to be ambitious again. It's time to shift our churches! Until the children of the almighty God act like His representatives on the earth, nothing will change in our countries. It does not matter how big our churches get or how wealthy they become or how beautiful we build them. The destiny of your land is in the hands of the church and her willingness to declare the position of God in the society.

NOT OF THIS WORLD?

Some people object to this teaching and quote John 18:36, where Jesus said, "My kingdom is not of this world...my kingdom is from another place." Christians have been using this phrase out of context for decades to forfeit this realm to Satan and neglect their calling to the nations. If His kingdom is not of this world, then we have no real assignment here except for evangelism and individual personal development. The hard work of restoring nations to the kingdom doesn't matter. These people turn Jesus's meaning on its head and twist His kingdom message into an antikingdom message.

Let's consider this passage in context. Pilate was quizzing Jesus about the source of Jesus's authority. He asked Him, "Are you the king of the Jews?...It was your people and your chief priests who handed you over to me" (John 18:33, 35). In response, Jesus said that His authority and assignment came from heaven, not from Earth. The Jews could not make Him a king; God the Father already had. Because men did not give Jesus His authority, they could not take it away from Him. He was operating with orders from a superior kingdom. That's why He said, "My kingdom is not of this world."

Did this mean He did not care about the earth? Of course not. The opposite is true. He came to Earth to bring the kingdom of God back to it. He cared about the world enough that He left a superior place and brought the superior principles of that place to a corrupted sphere. He wasn't saying He didn't care about the world, but that the world's kingdoms are not the source of His authority. Jesus's kingdom has everything to do with the earth and humanity, but it does not derive from them. "The one who comes from above is above all," Jesus said in John 3:31. He operates from above. So should we.

As followers of Jesus, our kingdom is not *of* this world, but that kingdom should rule this world here and now. Jesus specifically prayed that we would not be removed from the world (John 17). Jesus also said to occupy until He returns (Luke 19:13, KJV). Mark 1:15 and Luke 11:20 say the kingdom is at hand. It's here. It's now. It's what our lives are supposed to be about. And Daniel 2:44 says His kingdom will crush all others. The real focus of every Christian's life, and of all our church activities, is promoting the kingdom of God in every sphere of our nations. This was humanity's first mission, and it remains our primary mission.

OUR UNCHANGING MISSION

Our kingdom mandate predates the birth of Christ by thousands of years. God created this earth for mankind to rule. God said:

> Let us make man in our image, in our likeness, and let them rule over the fish of the sea and the birds of the air, over the livestock, over all the earth, and over all the creatures that move along the ground.
> **—Genesis 1:26**

God gave us this corner of the universe to reign, just as He is reigning over the universe. Adam was created in the image and after the likeness of God to rule the earth. He fellowshiped and communed with God; he dressed and kept the Garden of Eden. The glory of the kingdom was present in the Garden of Eden, and men were to multiply it. But when mankind sinned, we lost the glory of the kingdom. Catastrophe came to every sphere of life.

But God had a plan in place to restore the kingdom to earth as originally planned. Isaiah and Habakkuk prophesied that the glory of God would cover the earth again (Isa. 40:5; Hab. 2:14). That possibility returned to us with the arrival of Jesus, whose primary assignment was to restore the kingdom by restoring man's original purpose to us. The kingdom solves all problems. That's why John the Baptist said it was good news (Luke 3:18). The thing that was lost was coming back! Through the Second Adam—Jesus—God's original plan is being carried out, to have an earthly sphere entirely ruled by kingdom principles.

Think of it this way. When God created Adam, He put all nations in one person. All people who have ever lived came from Adam. You and I were in Adam. We share his DNA. His sin became our sin through inheritance (Rom. 5). God created a seed of a second Adam so all of us could become righteous through Him. In Jesus, God the Father put the ability to restore all nations. Jesus carried the redeemed nations in Him, spiritually speaking. That's why He could die for all nations, not just the Jews.

> Therefore, just as sin entered the world through one man, and death through sin, and in this way death came to all men, because all sinned.
>
> **—Romans 5:12**

God offered as a sacrifice His Son Jesus Christ in order to redeem the power and the authority from Satan and return dominion over the earth to man.

> For if, by the trespass of the one man, death reigned through that one man, how much more will those who receive God's abundant provision of grace and of the gift of righteousness reign in life through the one man, Jesus Christ. Consequently, just as the result of one trespass was condemnation for all men, so also the result of one act of righteousness was justification that brings life for all men.
>
> **—Romans 5:17–18**

God now expects us to move in the authority and power that Adam was originally given. We don't need to keep on looking at ourselves as if we are still not redeemed. No, we are back in Eden. Jesus said, "All authority in heaven and on earth has been given to me" (Matt. 28:18). Everyone who comes to Jesus and repents of his sins acquires the holiness, righteousness, power, and authority of Jesus Christ. He has transferred to us, His disciples, this power that He won back. That's why God calls us earthly kings and priests— because we are called to deliver this planet from evil (Rev. 5:10).

God will not supernaturally spread the kingdom, because that would rob man of his purpose. Spreading the kingdom is our job. The redemption of our friends, family, communities, and countrymen literally depends on the actions of the church. If the church doesn't start fighting corruption, it will keep flourishing in the country. If the church doesn't object to immorality, society will keep sliding more and more toward lawlessness. God wants the church to become the standard-bearer of order and righteousness in every country. As the apostle Peter wrote:

But you are a chosen people, a royal priesthood, a holy
nation, a people belonging to God, that you may declare
the praises of him who called you out of darkness into his
wonderful light.

—1 Peter 2:9

Salvation has made it possible for us to rule as Adam did.

BIG AMBITIONS

That's a big ambition, and any church that is focused on winning
its nation to God has big ambitions indeed. But a church that
is not focused on discipling nations exchanges big ambitions for
small ones without even realizing it. Many churches think they are
stretching themselves by building a new sanctuary or youth wing
or buying a church bus. But God's ambitions are vastly bigger. He
is sending Christians to impact entire societies. The promise of
God is that we can ask Him to give us the nations, not just a
bigger church building.

Sometimes my minister friends in America tell me how God is
blessing them by increasing attendance at their church and granting
them all sorts of earthly blessings. They tell me they're believing in
faith for a thousand more members, a new car, a television show,
and so on. I say, "If you want to use your faith to get a new car or
more church members, fine. But I'm using my faith to subdue and
change a nation." There is nothing wrong with houses and earthly
blessings, but those things are just tools. Some Christians become
satisfied with the tools. But the real reward is nations. God wants
to make many of us greater than we ever thought we would be.

Our ambitions need to match the size and scope of Christ's ambitions in coming to the earth. Did the only begotten Son of God humble Himself and come here to be violently and brutally murdered, hung on a cross, despised and mocked, then come back from the dead and preach and teach for forty days just so we could be prosperous and have emotion-stirring praise and worship times and pass out colorful leaflets and set up clever Web sites, all while people around us are depressed and committing suicide, spreading AIDS, dying of hunger, wrecking the planet, and much more? I think not.

I want to challenge you to lift your faith from small satisfactions. God will do more than pay your bills. That's what the Gentiles think about. God doesn't even call that a reward. Those things come automatically with salvation. Our ambition must be much bigger. We are part of the body of Christ whose members are called to restore the kingdom of God to Earth! The reward for seeking God is influence over a sphere of society so people can be rescued from the horrors of sin and evil. Anybody who walks in obedience to God has the right to ask for nations to be restored and given into his hands—and that very much includes you.

The time has come for us to remember the cross and the big ambitions Christ has for this planet. It is time to shift our thinking from hiding in church to ruling our promised lands for the glory of God. It's time for Christians to come into their inheritance, to discover their promised land. It's time to act, knock, and seek results. The time has come for the kingdom of God to be manifested so that the nations will follow God.

It is time to stop thinking of ourselves as occupying the bottom step of the social ladder. It is time to stop lying low. It is time to stop seeking redemption from influential people like politicians or tycoons. It is time to see ourselves as instruments in the hand of God. We are neither small nor insignificant, but God's messengers. He sees in you the destiny of your family, your friends, your co-workers, and your nation.

For a long time the church has taken care of itself only, but the time has come to take responsibility for every sphere of society, from our circle of friends to our families; from our workplaces to our city councils and schools; from sports and the arts to politics and business. Today the church needs to bring peoples and nations out of the desert, where they have been wandering. The kingdom of God is God's total answer to man's total problem. It is synonymous with God's will and ways. When He says, "Your kingdom come" (Luke 11:2), it means through you and me. We are to walk in power. Every gift and talent we have is to be exercised in service of the kingdom. Believers need to start social organizations and charities that will become strong social movements that captivate people's attention. We need to find effective ways to serve the homeless, the troubled, the orphan, the beaten, the addicted, the criminal, and the helpless.

God is waiting for us to take action. We don't have the moral right to be indifferent. God doesn't want a passive church.

One day our own nations will be judged. God will send some nations to hell as it says in Psalm 9:17 (NKJV):

> The wicked shall be turned into hell,
> And all the nations that forget God.

Let us work with all the skill and passion we have so that our nations will be saved.

25

As our church waited in the city square for the government's response to our protest, I could feel that change was coming to our country. We had cracked the ice. The deep freeze that had encased millions of souls for generations was beginning to thaw. Finally, the mayor of Kyiv came out of the building to address us personally. This was a wonderful surprise. He spoke through the megaphone and said the city would provide several hectares of land for us to build on. They would give us the land for free—a $5 million value. In return we promised to clear people from the streets so normal life could resume in Kyiv.

We had won a great victory. But we would soon discover that in a country like ours, victories like this could be short-lived. There was even greater turmoil to come than we had ever dreamed. And God was about to put us on the vanguard of a much bigger movement than we had bargained for.

KINGDOM PRINCIPLES
FROM CHAPTER 2

1. God eagerly awaits the redemption of the nations.

2. God wants preeminence in all things in every nation.

3. Until the children of the almighty God act like His representatives on the earth, nothing will change in our countries. The destiny of our countries is in the hands of the church and her willingness to declare the position of God in the society.

4. The real focus of every Christian's life and of all our church actvities is promoting the kingdom of God in every sphere of our nations.

5. If the church doesn't start fighting corruption, it will keep flourishing in the country.

6. A church that is not focused on discipling nations exchanges its big ambitions for small ones without even realizing it.

7. If you want to use your faith to get a new car or more church members, fine. But I'm using my faith to subdue and change a nation.

Chapter 3

FINDING YOUR
PROMISED LAND

THE FIRST THING PEOPLE WANT TO KNOW WHEN they begin to think in terms of changing society, culture, and whole nations is, "How do I get started? What is my part?" You have a specific promised land, the place where you are to exercise kingdom influence. I want to help you find your promised land and get started bringing the kingdom to the people and institutions around you.

Discovering your promised land is of primary importance. It is the gateway into kingdom effectiveness. In fact, I believe you will only be truly effective for God when you are working in your promised land. Many Christians in a variety of jobs and circumstances try to engage in individual evangelism whenever they can, but evangelism is only truly effective when you are operating in your area of gifting. A fish can't swim on the sidewalk. It has no grace there.

A person operating outside of his or her promised land is similarly clumsy. When you try to evangelize outside of your calling, it's unnatural. Nonbelievers don't like being imposed upon, and truthfully, no Christian likes imposing himself on others. It's miserable for everyone involved! But when you operate in your promised land, you are able to show God-given skill and provide kingdom answers, and people receive you with open arms. You gain standing with others. Their hearts become receptive to receive more from you. That is why to be an effective sharer of the gospel you must find your habitat, your promised land, where you are naturally graceful and fruitful. There you will use your gift effectively.

When I first arrived in Kyiv, Ukraine, I would ride around all day on a city bus weeping. I had no natural reason to be crying, but deep inside I felt both love and pain for this city, which would become intertwined with my kingdom destiny. I would sit in the bus crying out with my soul, "God, let this city bow before You." At times I would go to the tallest building in town, stand on the roof, and look across the cityscape. "God, let Your Spirit come!" I would pray.

In Ukraine, I had found my promised land. This was where God wanted to plant me and where I would have influence for His kingdom's sake.

Everything that God created has a particular function and a specific purpose—and that includes you. God gave you life and talents for a reason. You may not know what your purpose is, but that doesn't mean you don't have one. It just means you haven't found it yet. Each of us has the potential to become great. At one time in my life, I thought I was good for nothing and nothing would come of me. A lot of people think of themselves in the same way. But that is a lie of the devil. We are all good for something. And God has set aside tasks for us to do. If we don't do them, they may never get done.

How do you find your promised land? Here are several signposts to help you get there.

Find your promised land where love and pain intersect.

Your promised land is where your love and pain intersect. When I rode the bus around Kyiv, I felt great love and great pain for all I saw. My heart was enflamed and bound up in the city's future. Your concern and your pain can point the way to your promised land. When you feel pain and love for a particular problem or need in society, or for a particular place or people, this may be pointing you to your destiny. For example, some people look at their government and love it, but they feel pain at what the politicians are doing to the direction of their country. They want to bring righteousness to it. Moses felt that way. He loved his people and hated what the Egyptians were doing, so he killed a man. (See Exodus 2.) That murder was a work of the flesh, but it sprang from right motivation. His pain and love met in his concern for the Israelites.

Your promised land is where your passion lies. It is where your heart quickens, where you feel an almost supernatural hunger to intervene and improve a situation. Ask yourself these key questions that will help you to discover your promised land:

1. What do you love and enjoy doing? Sometimes what we call a hobby is really our calling.

2. What do you have passion for? What sets you on fire and consumes you with zeal?

3. What makes you angry and frustrated? What problems can you not get out of your head? You may be called to confront those problems with your talents and time.

Nobody can tell you for certain where your promised land is.

As a pastor I know firsthand that the diversity of gifts in the kingdom of God is much greater than any one person can understand or direct. No leader or pastor, friend or prophet, can tell you for certain where your promised land is, because no person can see everything God wants to do in society. It's not up to one person to set the agenda. That is the Holy Spirit's job. The leader's job is to empower people with kingdom principles and release them in confidence and strength.

Often people come up to me and share their burden or passion for an area of need that I did not know existed. For example, I did not know that sexual molestation was a problem until someone told me they wanted to minister to victims of molestation. Things I would never imagine are on the heart of God and need to be addressed. That is why He awakens the passion in each of us. If a leader tried to orchestrate kingdom activity, he would die trying and would never accomplish it anyway.

Finding your promised land is ultimately up to you and God.

Your gifts were made for others.

Your promised land will always involve meeting other people's needs. You might be a gifted leader or speaker, artist or mechanic, teacher or nurse. Each of these can become an incredibly fruitful area to bring the kingdom of God's influence. But by definition, your talents can only be useful when they bless others. Keep that focus in whatever you do. Your promised land is not about building you up or making you comfortable; it's about making you useful to others.

Your ministry is not limited to the pulpit.

It's a shame that some churches still teach that true ministry is limited to the pulpit. That's rubbish. Pulpit ministries are to help people discover and be effective in their own spheres of influence. But the vast majority of people are meant to serve outside the pulpit and the fivefold ministries. The engineers who attend my church are disguised evangelists, if you want to think of it that way. The politicians who attend my church are disguised apostles. The lawyers are disguised teachers. When you confine true ministry to the fivefold ministries, you make 95 percent of the church irrelevant.

Furthermore, your promised land is almost certainly not a ministry you feel you should start, but an actual place of influence in society that you can take back by the grace of God. Many Christians have become so religious that they are no longer passionate about what happens in the world. Because they have been locked up in the four walls of the church, their wildest desire is to become a preacher, evangelist, praise and worship leader, youth pastor, and so on. These are housekeeping ministries that need to be done excellently, but they should not be confused with the real work God has called the vast majority of believers to, which is in the world. Don't confuse the chore you perform in God's house for the promised land He gives you outside His house.

Break out of the mind-set that God only works through church leaders or church positions. Your ministry most likely takes place out in the world.

Your gift requires growth.

The Old Testament account of the Israelites leaving Egypt is an illustration for us. When we get saved and begin connecting to our kingdom purpose, we must go through a growth process. You will not take your promised land suddenly and all at once. God told the Israelites:

> The LORD your God will drive out those nations before you, little by little. You will not be allowed to eliminate them all at once, or the wild animals will multiply around you.
>
> —Deuteronomy 7:22

It will take a while to fully take over the piece of the promised land you are meant to subdue through the talents God gave you. Expect it to take time, and expect to grow along the way.

Destruction and boredom are signs you are missing your promised land.

Ignorance of your promised land is dangerous because it leads to ruin and destruction. But knowledge gives freedom. That's why Jesus said, "Then you will know the truth, and the truth will set you free" (John 8:32). The truth on its own cannot make you free. Only knowledge of the truth can set you free.

Misuse is the same as destruction. The Bible says, "My people are destroyed from lack of knowledge" (Hos. 4:6). Ignorance and lack of knowledge can be the cause of a Christian's ruin.

I have taught our people for years that they are not just waiting to go to heaven but that God has called them for a purpose. As a result, everyone in our church knows their purpose in life. They are either thriving in that purpose or are training to be effective in it. Finding your promised land will do more than anything else to quell self-destructive tendencies and boredom.

If you are obedient to God and do what He has created you to do, then your task will fill up your life. You won't have time to be self-destructive or bored.

Sometimes what you train for isn't your calling.

My calling is to be a minister, but for a while I wanted to become a journalist. I studied for six years in the university and received two degrees in journalism. But my kingdom calling was not to be a journalist. Had I followed that course and become a journalist, I would have never been so fulfilled, accomplished, and happy as I am now. I was trained in one area, but my promised land was in a different area altogether.

Sometimes your calling lies outside your training. God will use circumstances to train you, but be ready to go in new directions as God leads you. Do not resist a change in direction. If a man is called to be a doctor, but he insists on being a businessman, he will be miserable and of little use to God. If a woman is called to be a business leader but is working as a teacher, she will not be totally fulfilled. They will be like the fig tree that bears no fruit.

> Seeing a fig tree by the road, he went up to it but found nothing on it except leaves. Then he said to it, "May you never bear fruit again!" Immediately the tree withered.
> —**Matthew 21:19**

Be faithful with little.

Because we take over our promised lands gradually, we must show ourselves faithful at each step. Before the next stage in your calling opens up to you, you will have to go through times of waiting and preparation. During these times you learn to be faithful in what is least. So your place of calling becomes your place of manifesting Christ as a servant.

> Whoever can be trusted with very little can also be trusted with much, and whoever is dishonest with very little will also be dishonest with much.
> —**Luke 16:10**

This may also include a season of serving in another person's promised land. If you have not found your own promised land, or if you are still in training, don't stand idly by, but help others find their promised lands. Our goal in subduing our own promised land is not about self-fulfillment or self-advancement. Rather, we have a common cause with other kingdom-minded believers, and we must help each other as much as our time and training will allow. Nobody can excuse themselves from labor simply because they do not know where their promised land is. Let us help one another. Ours is a common goal, not a one-man show. Help your colaborers, just as you wish to be helped by them to be effective in your promised land.

HEAR FROM GOD

The other major key to finding your promised land is to look beyond the natural. Go to God and ask Him for what purpose He created you. God is your maker, and He's the only One who fully knows your purpose and calling in life. To proceed without His direct input is foolish.

How does God speak to us? He has given us His Word as a plumb line for each one of us. But when God wants to give you personal guidance concerning a specific matter, He will make certain parts of His Word come alive and become a source of revelation for you. God can lead you through your whole life by means of His Word, by speaking to you in dreams or through sermons, by warning you through prophecies, or advising you through other people or through books you read. God has many different ways of communicating with us. The secret of Jesus's successful life and ministry was that He frequently communed with God and always followed His advice.

> I do nothing on my own but speak just what the Father
> has taught me. The one who sent me is with me; he has
> not left me alone, for I always do what pleases him.
>
> —John 8:28–29

Take note of that. What did Jesus do? Only those things that He learned from His Father. Reach out in prayer to get an understanding of God's plan, of His revelation and vision for your life. Expect God to speak to you. Ask Him specific questions. Thank Him for the answers in advance. Sometimes His answer comes while you are reading the Bible; sometimes it can be an inward witness, a joy or a heaviness in your heart; or sometimes He speaks to us through our circumstances. God has many ways of getting information into a man's heart and mind so He can develop a right understanding of a situation.

Always remember: do only what you have seen with your spiritual eyes. If you learn to live in this way, you will rarely stumble. Jesus said:

> By myself I can do nothing; I judge only as I hear, and my
> judgment is just, for I seek not to please myself but him
> who sent me.
>
> —John 5:30

Get Educated

Once you have found your promised land, go and fully explore it. In the Bible, Moses sent spies to search out the Promised Land for the people of Israel. They spent forty days there, studying the terrain, investigating the people and crops. This is a model for us to follow.

The best way to explore your promised land is through education. For a long time many Christians thought that they could get away with reading the Bible only and not bothering with an education. That is why Christians have lost their edge to the ungodly in almost every sphere of life. People who have cultivated professionalism, service, and excellence have taken over, even if they do not belong to the kingdom of God. We have acted like fools, thinking that the anointing of God would carry us through. The Bible says:

> Every prudent man acts out of knowledge, but a fool exposes his folly.
>
> **—Proverbs 13:16**

> Blessed is the man who finds wisdom, the man who gains understanding.
>
> **—Proverbs 3:13**

We must maximize our abilities by educating ourselves. Each of us needs a program of self-education. Research your area of gifting, read about it, exhaust the literature and teaching materials. Make yourself a lifelong learner so you can be a sharp arrow in God's hands. As it says:

> He made my mouth like a sharpened sword,
>   in the shadow of his hand he hid me;
> he made me into a polished arrow
>   and concealed me in his quiver.
>
> **—Isaiah 49:2**

Every Christian is called to be a polished shaft in God's quiver. You are His weapon. The sharp end of an arrow symbolizes its focus on the target and its excellence in penetrating problems. Through education you become a powerful weapon in the hands of God.

But self-education alone is not enough. An indispensable way to sharpen yourself is by going to the best schools and becoming a recognized specialist and professional in your area of endeavor. Universities have several advantages over self-education. They teach you to have discipline to study, research, and meet deadlines. They broaden your knowledge and bring you into contact with people of diverse experiences. And a university gives you a diploma that people will recognize. This gives you credibility in the eyes of men.

If you try to take your promised land without getting an education, you are doomed to failure. On the other hand, diligent training and education in your field of specialization secure your success. Apply maximum effort because you are working not just for yourself but to transform a nation by shifting from where you are. Do all you can to acquire knowledge. Knowledge is one of God's primary ways of dispelling darkness, evil, and ignorance. Knowledge guarantees eventual success. It focuses your efforts. Keep striving to perfect yourself in your field, and press on to learn as much as you can.

A kingdom education

As a Christian, you have an additional advantage and responsibility when taking your promised land. Knowledge alone will not exalt a nation. Knowledge must lead to righteousness. Like Daniel in the Bible, you must combine professional knowledge with knowledge of kingdom principles like integrity, holiness, love, and compassion. Because you have the mind of Christ, you are called to pair your natural learning with spiritual knowledge and wisdom. You can see all aspects of a problem, not just the earthly aspect. As you study, you will see the gaps in what secular sources are teaching you, because you have higher truth. That enables you to generate an even better approach to problems in your area of expertise.

For example, at the university where I studied, I learned in my sociology class that society could be divided into spheres—government, sports, the arts, business, and so on. That thought became the foundation for how our church now takes the principles of the kingdom of God to society. We focus on those specific areas, just as I learned in school.

Another thing I learned when studying modern civilization is that the reforms brought about by Martin Luther and the Protestant Reformation form the basis of today's society. Protestant values are what people in the West live by, and that is why the West has had so much success in creating peaceful, wealthy societies. Historians and scientists all agree that the teaching of the Protestant preachers were directly responsible for today's civilization. For example, a desire to spread the gospel led to the invention of the printing press. The same values led to the invention of the modern-day banking and credit systems; time and clocks; democratic systems of government; modern industrial systems; the rule of law; equal and balanced systems of wealth distribution; and the Protestant work ethic. The Protestants are also responsible for the tradition of debt settlement, marriage as the institution of one man and one woman, obeying parents, weekends and church attendance on Sundays. Even if some of these things were practiced before, the Protestants elevated them to a level of worldwide influence.

By seeing how biblical principles led to stability, health, and wealth in the past, I get fresh ideas about how to change societies today. I combine kingdom purposes with my knowledge of history.

At the university I also began to discern that nations do not become great by the virtue of their wealth, but by the wealth of their virtues. For example, Switzerland has few natural resources compared to most countries in Africa. But it is a much healthier, wealthier, and more just and stable country than any country in Africa. Switzerland's wealth is in its moral fabric and the value system of her people. (See Isaiah 59.) She has made much more of her comparatively meager resources than any African country has made with its great natural wealth.

Even reading about the Bolshevik Revolution gave me ideas and inspiration. That revolution led to much evil, but I saw how one man, V. I. Lenin, was able to change the history of a whole country. I am one man. I can change a whole country too! And so can you, by combining your education with kingdom wisdom and knowledge.

For many years our church has encouraged people to get educated and obtain degrees. The Embassy of God even has educational programs such as the Center for Business Transformation, the Institute of Personality Development, the Institute for Transformation of Society, a linguistic center, and more. We want even the structure of our church programs to point people outside and to encourage them to get further education. That's what it will take to fully impact Ukraine for Christ.

Today, members of our church work in all spheres of the society, taking an active position for the kingdom and excelling in their work. We have many people of all ages who are now students at various universities. Many are members of social organizations that actively influence the social issues in the country. Many are active in business. Just a few years ago some of these people were unemployed, but now they are citizen leaders of the country. They are people of honor and influence. This didn't happen by a miracle. It happened by finding their promised lands and exploring them fully.

Education is a never-ending process. On the spiritual side you must continually study the Bible and other Christian books and sermons. In your area of giftedness you must keep up with the advancing knowledge or you risk losing your influence and becoming a dull arrow. Even if you already hold a position of authority, stay ahead of the rest by constantly searching out and studying the new developments.

Remember: misuse, ruin, and destruction are inevitable where there is no knowledge. Knowledge, understanding, and wisdom enable kings to reign effectively. Jesus studied His Father constantly, and He told His disciples:

> I tell you the truth, the Son can do nothing by himself; he can do only what he sees his Father doing, because whatever the Father does the Son also does.
>
> **—John 5:19**

Education and wisdom were the secrets to Jesus's dominion: He acquired wisdom from observing the Father and acting likewise. It is the same for you and me. Nobody can go further than their knowledge. Seek knowledge and understanding and all obstacles will be removed from your way. Every situation will bow its knees before the revelation of God.

Seeking Egypt's help

But don't mistake getting knowledge with adopting the world's ways. When your life goal is to build a big church or ministry, it's possible to be wrapped up in it so much that you begin to play the world's games. The Bible warns against this.

> Woe to those who go down to Egypt for help,
>> who rely on horses,
> who trust in the multitude of their chariots
>> and in the great strength of their horsemen,
> but do not look to the Holy One of Israel,
>> or seek help from the LORD.
> Yet he too is wise and can bring disaster;
>> he does not take back his words.
> He will rise up against the house of the wicked,
>> against those who help evildoers.
> But the Egyptians are men and not God;
>> their horses are flesh and not spirit.
> When the LORD stretches out his hand,
>> he who helps will stumble,
>> he who is helped will fall;
>> both will perish together.
>
> —Isaiah 31:1–3

Egypt is symbolic of the world, and God is warning us not to strengthen ourselves in the world's ways or put ourselves under the world's yoke. There is a big difference between seeking the world's knowledge and taking on the world's character. It is worthless and senseless to seek spiritual help in Egypt. Help comes from the Lord who created heaven and Earth. If God sends us to "Egypt," it is to learn certain principles, not to be conformed to its character.

The Prison of the Pew

Since I started preaching this message of "churchshift" around the world, church members often tell me they feel trapped in the pews of their churches. One husband and wife wrote this to me:

> We have served on the staff of churches. But as regular church members now, we have been frustrated at the lack of ministry opportunity. We see that others share the same sense of discouragement. These are people who love the Lord and have a burning passion for ministry in their hearts, but for the most part go unrecognized, unempowered, and often misunderstood by church leadership.
>
> Many people desperately want their relationship with God, leadership skills, talents, and life experience to count for the kingdom, but their experience has been that few pastors and leaders know how to embrace and empower them to become ministers outside the four walls of the church.
>
> So, people leave their abilities and skills outside the door while they worship and fellowship with other believers. When they leave, they again pick up their leadership roles. This has created a trend now where gifted people leave the organized church and unite in home group settings.
>
> Those with a more define and focused ministry vision form parachurch ministries rather than defending their already proven leadership abilities before a church board. These people are often labeled rebellious renegades. Though their ministries may be flourishing, they are flourishing right outside the walls of their home church.
>
> If people adhere to the basic tenets of faith and have servant's hearts, there should be nothing that stops ministry

from flowing freely from every believer throughout the body of Christ as long as the church's ministry structure and chain authority is respected and understood by all.

It has long been our desire to see all the resources God has placed within the hearts and lives of believers turned loose on an unsuspecting world. Let us not become permission-withholding Pharisees who stifle the gifts, skills, and talents of the very people God sent to help us. Let us become compassionate, permission-granting spiritual leaders.

Ironically, professionals in politics, entertainment, sports, and other spheres of society have taken their company's message worldwide in a way the church has not been able to for two thousand years. Globally, Mickey Mouse is a more recognized name than Jesus Christ. In many places the shape of the Coca-Cola bottle is more recognized than the cross. The debut of Apple's iPhone swept the world in a single day. Yet when professionals from those industries come to our churches, we typically ask them to give their tithes and perhaps do some housekeeping services such as serving on the board or teaching a class. How much more quickly could we finish the Great Commission if we tapped into the vast resource of people who sit like prisoners in our pews.

Pastors need to train and teach their members to stop being pew warmers and to become a people called out of the world's lifestyle to subdue every sphere of their lives to God and the kingdom principles. This is such a crucial matter that we will spend the next chapter discussing how to become kingdom minded.

KINGDOM PRINCIPLES
FROM CHAPTER 3

1. Your promised land will always involve meeting other people's needs.

2. When you confine true ministry to the fivefold ministries, you make 95 percent of the church irrelevant.

3. Don't confuse the chore you perform in God's house with the promised land He gives you outside His house.

4. Your place of calling becomes your place of manifesting Christ as a servant.

5. The best way to explore your promised land is through education.

6. Knowledge must lead to righteousness.

7. Nobody can go further than their knowledge.

Chapter 4

BECOMING
KINGDOM MINDED

A SHIFT MUST OCCUR. BEFORE WE CAN RULE in our promised land, we must be ruled by the kingdom. The Bible calls this being "transformed by the renewing of your mind" (Rom. 12:2). If we want a new nation, we must shift as individuals. We will only find success in transforming our workplace, our families, our social sphere, and our society as we abide by kingdom rules. Jesus said it this way:

> I am the vine; you are the branches. If a man remains in me and I in him, he will bear much fruit; apart from me you can do nothing.
>
> —John 15:5

God was on our side the day we openly challenged the government. The newspapers and all the people were astonished at the result. We had stared down the leaders of our country—and won. The effects on the country would be more momentous than we had even dreamed. And through that single act we received more coverage nationwide than in the ten years we had sat in our church praying and fasting.

God also will be on the side of everyone who uses kingdom principles—and this is your calling as a child of God. The Bible tells us something amazing about God:

> For You have magnified Your word above all Your name.
> —**Psalm 138:2**, NKJV

That is an amazing statement. God has elevated His kingdom principles (His Word) above even His name. His principles cannot be circumvented. He will not violate them just because you pray. That would be God working against Himself, and a kingdom divided will not stand. He will not do you special favors. Rather, it is our task to become kingdom minded.

To do this, we must do more than find our promised land. We must embody the King. We must be fully impacted by His nature so that we have His nature. The very word *kingdom* means "king's domain." Christ's kingdom is made up of two things: Christ's nature and Christ's rule. But His nature must come first. I like to tell people they must be addicted to God. A kingdom addiction is the only addiction we are allowed in this life. (See 1 Corinthians 16:15.) When we embody the characteristics and values of Christ the King and live by His teachings and principles, we actually bring the lifestyle of the kingdom of God to our world.

THE ILLS OF A CHURCH-MINDED CHURCH

Matthew 6:33 tells us the only thing we should seek after is the advancement and victory of God's kingdom and the triumph of His righteousness over the unrighteousness of the world. But many people in the church are more church minded than kingdom minded. I have observed that when a church neglects the Great Commission mandate to transform nations, it falls into several predictable traps.

In-fighting

Too much light burns the eyes. Too much salt burns the tongue. When Christians make church the focal point of their lives and ministry, they burn each other like an oversalted dish and blind each other like a room full of spotlights.

Salt and light are not meant for themselves. We are not called the salt of the church but the salt of the earth (Matt. 5:13). We are not called the light of the church but the light of the world (Matt. 5:14). The more you stay in the saltshaker or under the bushel, the less salty you become and the dimmer grows your light. Even worse, you become more prone to fight with other believers.

When a church loses focus, people get busy fighting among themselves. When our eyes slip from our kingdom purpose, we abuse the institutions Jesus wants to use to bring kingdom life to the earth.

As a child in Nigeria, I found salt on the street one day. I collected it, brought it home, and used the salt to prepare some food. I tasted the food, but it didn't taste the least bit salty. I salted it again, but still there was no change in the taste. Then I poured almost all the salt into the pot, but still there was no change. I finally tasted the salt and found it had no taste at all.

I asked my grandmother about this, and she told me that this salt had lost its saltiness because it had gone too long without being used. This sounds like some believers and churches. They go too long without being used. The Bible says, "It is no longer good for anything, except to be thrown out and trampled by men" (Matt. 5:13).

Recently I heard about a meeting of pastors where this truth struck such a powerful chord that they came up with a joint statement of apology to people in their churches. It read:

> As pastors and ministry leaders within the local church, we have believed and operated with the mind-set that all ministries were church related and that they were to be under its government and control. We have not understood the kingdom of God or how it was to manifest on the earth. As a result we have used people to build our churches and ministries. In doing so we have not honored those called by God to minister in commerce, media, arts, government, social services, and most other occupations outside the influence of the organized church. If individuals could not or would not serve our vision for our churches, we undervalued them as less important—but

accepting them as sources of income. Most of these people have been ignored, and as a result they have become discouraged and disconnected. Many have left in frustration, anger, and disillusionment, believing somehow that they were less spiritual. Others have given up trying to fit themselves into the limited space within the local church structure and ministry. We have attempted to make business executives into intercessors, sales people into children's nursery workers, business administrators into Sunday school superintendents, and so the list goes on and on.

As pastors and ministry leaders, we want to tell you that we have been wrong. What we have taught and demonstrated for generations within the church has been shallow and selfish. We are sincerely sorry, and we come in repentance for our bad attitudes, wrong beliefs, and our poor behavior towards you. Please forgive us. We honor you as kingdom people, called by God to the marketplace. We believe you are ordained by God to occupy and to transform your sphere of influence and the territory to which you have been called. We release honor, blessing, and favor on your life and personal calling to the marketplace. We as pastors and ministry leaders are prepared to stand with you and support you in your God-given ministries. You have dreams ordained by God. It is our privilege and heart's desire to call them forth and to see you fully established in the destiny for your life.[1]

I believe this could be the confession of most churches of today. Until we equip and release people we will never impact society. A church that has an outward-looking kingdom focus simply has no bored people. Everybody is busy in the proper direction. Everybody is fulfilling their purpose and subduing their promised land. Nobody has time for internal squabbles or unimportant questions. They see clearly. Their focus is on the earth, not on the church. There are no power struggles because the church is no longer the prize. People are too busy learning to impact the world in their unique, God-given way.

Egocentric leadership

I was in Seattle recently and saw Bill Gates and his wife go into a coffee shop. They had only one bodyguard with them. I was amazed!

Yet I have seen big-time pastors in the United States travel with squads of bodyguards. You can't get close to them. They don't possess even 1 percent of the wealth Bill Gates has, yet they prance around like kings. Having met with billionaires and famous people, I have found it is actually easier to approach many of them than it is to approach some pastors. God help us!

Sometimes our eyes slip from the kingdom and fall onto ourselves. When our focus is not on finding our promised land and changing our society from right where we are, we start using kingdom resources to build our own kingdoms. We become egocentric.

One of the biggest symptoms of egocentric leadership is the church ownership mentality. When a pastor refers to "my church" and "my people," he often betrays his true feelings. He sees the church as his flock, even his bride—and the measure of his career success.

I used to behave like a church owner until God taught me a hard lesson. I had planted a church in Belarus as a very young man and tended it as carefully as if it were my child. But one day God told me to give it up and help another group start a church. It was hard to leave that first little church, but I did it in obedience. I helped form a second church, and I often preached. We started a Bible school in the church, and I thought I would be ministering there for many years. But less than a year later, God told me to withdraw from ministry and sit in the congregation during the meetings. I was perplexed and disappointed. To start a church is an enormous task. I had put so much effort into it. Everyone looked to me as their teacher and as a person with authority. But again I was obedient to God and became an ordinary church member. God raised up one of the other members of the group to be the pastor.

A year passed, and God spoke to me about starting another church with some local students. I obeyed again and started this third church, but shortly thereafter God spoke to me again and said, "Leave this church too." I did, and less than a year later God began insisting again that I start a new church in a different location. I finally replied, "I'm not going to start any new churches." I was afraid He would tell me to leave it again after a month or two. I didn't know if I could take the heart-wrenching experience of giving up another church. I didn't understand it at the time, but through these trials and experiences God was teaching me to let go of His bride.

In my confusion, God answered me gently but firmly. He impressed on my heart that there was one thing He wanted me never to forget. I was not to build my own kingdom. There are people who claim to be nondenominational, but in reality they are building their own kingdom. He wanted me always to understand that He alone is the Lord of the church. Whether there are ten people in it or hundreds of thousands, this church would always be His. I had no claim over it. God could take me away from it whenever He wished, so I needed to be prepared for this at any time.

That settled the matter in my mind. Today, I could leave my church and become an ordinary member of its congregation or get involved in something quite different without the slightest regret, sorrow, or inner pain. I tell you this from the depth of my heart, because earlier I experienced real pain. But now I know that the church is not mine.

Too many church leaders talk about "my ministry" and "my church." I have heard men weep and plead with God, "O Lord! Do this or that in my church." They are trying to bribe God with their tears. They would make God a mere means to fulfill their own dreams. They are church minded, not kingdom minded.

The author of life said only one thing is worth thinking about: the kingdom. Nothing else should compete with it for our attention. Build the kingdom and be faithful to the church, but don't get attached to the church. Cling only to the kingdom and the King. We do not own the church. We are simply God's co-workers. Everyone from the most well-known church leader to the "lowliest" layperson must have the same attitude. We are not the owners but the laborers.

Think of it this way. The church is Jesus's bride. In John 21 Jesus told Peter, in essence, "Love me, and feed the flock." The bride belongs to Jesus, not you. Love Him first. If the church is Jesus's bride, then we are not allowed to love the church. That would be committing spiritual adultery. Husbands are to love their wives and the Lord, not Jesus's bride. Jesus said to love Him, but only feed or care for the church.

Size focus

Egocentric churches love to focus on numbers. When a church gets big enough, its pastors and congregation members have a smugness about them. At every opportunity they boast about having large crowds at their churches.

It's OK to talk numbers and to rejoice in God's blessing of numerical growth, but it's childish to revel in it and compare ourselves with others. If a church grows in numbers, the point is to glorify Christ, that His name might become known all over the world, that everyone might grow into the measure of the stature of the fullness of Christ.

I pastor a large church, but it's not a big deal to me, and it's not my goal. It's just a platform God has given us as a group to impact our nation. When a church is strong or large, there are fewer barriers for it. People will respect and honor you simply because you are a member of that church. That kind of influence can help people establish the kingdom of God more effectively. But there is absolutely no use in having a big church without changing the culture, speaking to society, and curing social ills.

Egocentric followers

Egocentric leaders produce egocentric followers. When a pastor is using a church to meet his own needs, this motivation trickles down to people in the pew who begin to see the church as existing to meet their personal needs. A culture of self-gratification grips the church. People go there to get a feel-good message. They get caught up in living for themselves, wanting a career and blessings and influence. They get a warped view of church and believe it exists to give them a positive weekly experience and tools for personal success. They forget that the reason we are alive and saved is to have maximum impact for Him by transforming our nations.

As kingdom people we are not free moral agents anymore. We are on duty to transform the earth for the Lord. You and I are not here to have a good job, or a good house, or to be healed and delivered so we can recreate and relax. Deuteronomy 6:23 says He brought them out of Egypt with a purpose that He might bring them into the land of promise. The land of promise will be conquered and filled with the glory of the Lord. Each one of us has his own piece of the earth to subdue, his own land of promise. We have an assignment from God to be His reformer. That's why you and I were saved. He needs someone to be His feet, hands, and character to righteously subdue and manage an area that was previously ruled by ungodliness. We are to reclaim and change the world, not use its resources to meet our own desires.

Your job is not just a job. It's a platform God has given you to change society. It is not about your salary, but about promoting the kingdom of God. You were created for this, to win the earth back to God piece by piece. When a church has God's ambitions you don't hear people say, "Pray for my depression. Pray I'll get a raise. Pray I'll get a bigger house. Pray for me, me, me." People who are on a kingdom mission tend to forget about their problems.

Egocentrism kills leadership because it shrinks their ambitions to the size of their own desires. It kills people in the pew by drawing their attention away from kingdom work and toward themselves.

Lack of purpose

I spoke with a pastor of an American megachurch recently. His church has fifteen thousand people. He told me, "I can walk into the mayor's office any time I want, but I don't know what to tell him." What an indictment. Yet many churches that are supposedly doing a great work are in a similar situation. They interact with society without changing it. But it's not enough to socialize with the world or to grow impressively large congregations so that community leaders speak well of us. We must permeate, influence, and change the society.

I learned this lesson after my church grew to fifteen thousand people. Everybody was applauding me for having a big church in such an unlikely place, but the praise was all about me and us. It felt terribly wrong, and we were in danger of losing our focus.

My focus was restored when I read Isaiah 49:8 (NKJV):

In an acceptable time I have heard You,
And in the day of salvation I have helped You;
I will preserve You and give You
As a covenant to the people,
To restore the earth,
To cause them to inherit the desolate heritages.

It hit me that God wants the earth restored back to Him. If we grew our church to a million people but didn't change society, we would have failed in our mission. It would be like building a big corporation like Microsoft, or a popular social club. That truth transformed my mind. Before then my goal was to get as many as possible saved and into heaven by bringing them into the church.

But our goal is supposed to be different. We can send people into the world like mustard seeds so that the kingdom, which Jesus compares to a highly invasive plant, will spread and take over.

Churches that lose kingdom focus lack purpose. They may have large crowds, large buildings, renown, and wealth, but they don't know how to use them.

Teaching fragments of the truth

Some churches get caught up in teaching one particular aspect of the kingdom of God while neglecting others. Some churches and ministers emphasize healing; others, prosperity, family values, prayer, the baptism in the Holy Spirit, salvation, and so on. Each of these is part of the truth, but none of them alone is the whole truth. Unless a church continually and relentlessly pursues a total kingdom agenda, it's easy to fall into teaching only fragments of the truth. For example, some churches preach the gospel of salvation without teaching about transforming society. They get people saved but do not train them in any relevant activity. They preach one aspect of the kingdom. But the kingdom and its gospel is a totality. The gospel of salvation, in isolation, will not change the earth.

When you teach a half-truth you destroy the truth. The saying goes, "A half-truth is a whole lie." Half-truth is as dangerous if not more dangerous than the absence of truth. That's why some people despise the church. They see religious people focused on one aspect of the truth, and they are turned off. Believe it or not, people outside the kingdom want to join the kingdom. They know instinctively that there is life in being kingdom minded. Life without God is senseless, and people understand this. But they need someone to show them how the kingdom works. They are like people trying to charge a cell phone by setting it on a stovetop and turning on the heat. They have the right idea—trying to get energy and electricity into the telephone—but they are destroying the phone as a result. In the same way they destroy their lives by being ignorant of the kingdom of God. As a kingdom citizen you have the answer. You can tell people how life works. But they don't want a sliver of the truth. They want the whole package.

Jesus brought a total gospel, the salvation of man and his surroundings. Our churches must also have a total kingdom message to change whole society, including crime, poverty, stewardship of the earth, business, the arts, the governments, and many other spheres. We can't major on certain issues and minor on others. Our message must be comprehensive. Our enemies attack us because we preach half the gospel, and they are right to do so. If the church stands only for certain truths, it will be seen as hypocritical. Partial truth leads to injustice. Jesus asks us to disciple nations with the whole truth.

HOW TO BE KINGDOM MINDED

To be kingdom minded is to reject the world's way of thinking and to live by superior principles from a superior place. The kingdom to which Christians belong is superior. The principles we live by are superior. Love is superior to hatred. Mercy is superior to vengeance. (See James 2:13.) Honesty is superior to dishonesty. These are some of the weapons we use in our promised lands.

This world can only be properly managed by people who rule from a superior place and superior principles. Only good can overcome evil—this is one of the most important laws on Earth. Paul wrote, "Do not be overcome by evil, but overcome evil with good" (Rom. 12:21). Good is more powerful than evil. I earlier quoted John 3:31, which says, "The one who comes from above is above all." That is our position too. We are seated in heavenly realms with Christ. That means that we rule from His position of superiority. What makes Him superior? His nature and principles that God has exalted above His name. Those same principles make us kingdom minded.

There is no way to properly rule and subdue the earth by using principles of the kingdom of darkness. The people of this world walk in the futility of their minds. They cannot understand what it means to "Love your enemies, bless those who curse you, do good to those who hate you" (Matt. 5:44, NKJV). They are stuck with a set of inferior principles, and they get inferior results. God did not design the human body for things like fornication, envy, theft, indecent language, irritation, anger, and alcohol and drug addiction. He designed our minds and bodies to function by kingdom principles. To hate is to slowly self-destruct. To manipulate others is to invite death into your life. It's against how your mind and body were made. Evil cannot overcome evil. Bodies, brains, and spirits were meant to function on kingdom principles. The Bible says:

> So I tell you this, and insist on it in the Lord, that you must no longer live as the Gentiles do, in the futility of their thinking. They are darkened in their understanding and separated from the life of God because of the ignorance that is in them due to the hardening of their hearts.
> —Ephesians 4:17–18

To change and improve the world you must have a superior position and superior principles. You can only transform something if you are not conformed to it (Rom. 12:2). The principles of the kingdom are no secret. They are found throughout the Bible, particularly in the Gospels where they are perfectly embodied in Christ. The principles include love, peace, justice, mercy, goodness, gentleness, unity, compassion, and holiness. These are superior to what the world operates by, which is control, power, hatred, manipulation, division, threats, revenge, greed, and selfishness. Though the principles of darkness may seem powerful to us at times, they are inferior principles. They break down in the presence of kingdom-minded people. They are the rules of a doomed power structure.

To rule properly is to embody the King's nature. Jesus encouraged us to "let your light shine before men, that they may see your good deeds and praise your Father in heaven" (Matt. 5:16). We are called by God to "live such good lives among the pagans that, though they accuse you of doing wrong, they may see your good deeds and glorify God on the day he visits us" (1 Pet. 2:12). Our holiness and righteousness is the best testimony we have for showing people that God is real. No matter how they behave toward us or what they say about us, there will come a time when people see our good works and understand what holiness, virtue, and the love of God are about. We must work better and harder than anybody else. We must respect all people. We must be the best in every area of our lives. We must continue doing good, because good will always overcome evil in the end.

In your area of calling, apply those principles, using them to demonstrate the kingdom of God for everyone to see. Embody sincerity, honesty, truth, integrity, and hard work. By the business you build and how you conduct yourself you are actually building the kingdom through your life. It becomes a glaring example of righteousness and a model for the world to see and emulate. We are to thrust ourselves into the world because that is where we set people free. We don't run from problems; we run to them. Light doesn't run from darkness but the other way around. We are problem chasers! We have the answer for every problem in the world. That is our Great Commission calling—through active application of kingdom principles.

Many people come to the Embassy of God who are directors of companies, and they often ask me, "How should we deal with Christians who are working for us and who are unreliable, undisciplined, and sluggardly?" My feeling is that anyone who has that kind of attitude to his job is simply not a Christian. Christians must be the first and best in everything; they must be transparent examples of virtuous living.

> For it is God's will that by doing good you should silence
> the ignorant talk of foolish men.
> —**1 Peter 2:15**

Living by kingdom principles is in our best interests. It's not about becoming religious. It's about having your ability to rule over this world restored. As a young believer I used to think that by obeying God's Word and commandments I was simply pleasing God. But today I understand that obeying God's Word and commandments is actually to my benefit. It keeps me from self-destruction. It helps me to establish authority over my promised land.

Forget what it's like to have hatred, anger, and unforgiveness in your heart. These are foreign to us as Christians. They slip right off us as if we were made of Teflon. Our hearts and minds are consumed with better things. Our commitment to the kingdom is our food, our treasure, our life. Remember: the kingdom of God will work for us at the same level we are committed to the kingdom.

REPENTANCE

The problem for many people is they don't fully reject the principles of this world. They establish partial friendship with the world. They try to mix kingdoms. They use principles of the kingdom of darkness to establish their rule. They use secrecy, anger, dishonesty, and worse. The prince of this world, who is the devil, directs their actions without their realizing it. Meanwhile, they believe they are the ones in charge. They believe they are doing God's work, but they are using inferior principles and falling into the futility of their minds.

Children of God have nothing to learn from people who walk in darkness, and there is no need to imitate them! Friendship with the world is enmity with God. There is no middle ground.

Perhaps you have accepted Christ but are not overcoming the world because you are not fully identified with His kingdom. To rule effectively you must be enveloped and engulfed by kingdom principles. Your affections must be set on things above. You cannot rule with half commitment. It must penetrate your brain and your soul. There must be no room for anything else.

Many preachers don't preach repentance, but Jesus did. (See Mark 1:15.) There will always be the need to repent, even when you are living in the kingdom. To repent means to change your mind and your belief system as often as needed. It is the process we go through to become kingdom minded. We repent because the kingdom of heaven is here. It is about rejecting the old and embracing the new. It's about again embracing the benefits of that superior kingdom, which provides protection, guidance, health, prosperity, and purpose. There is no life apart from the kingdom. When we find the King and repent of our old ways and commit to embody His nature, we can rule our promised lands.

LOVE

If I could sum up kingdom-mindedness in one word, it would be *love*. I used to think it was not possible to love all people equally. But I discovered the secret of how to do it, and today I really do love all people. I reached that place of love through a difficult realization. One day God told me to listen to my own sermons on tape because I was teaching principles that I did not fully embody. So I put all my sermons together and started listening to them and reading through all my notes. I started memorizing the Word and meditating on it.

During one particular two-month period I concentrated on 1 Corinthians 13, the love chapter. I prayed and meditated over it. I knew in theory that love is not provoked, yet I was often provoked. I meditated on how to apply that Word in different situations. I asked myself, "What if someone punches me or spits into my face? Will I be provoked then?" I found out that my knowledge was still theory, so I took the Word again and "replayed" it in my mind until theory was transformed into practice. By the time I finished that exercise, I found I had become a different person. I could no longer be provoked. I grew to love not only the members of my church but also my enemies and those who plotted evil against me. I can now boast that there is no one I don't like in my life. I can no longer be angry or irritated. God doesn't have these qualities. He looks at people with love. His love fills my heart, and therefore I love everybody no matter how they treat me.

Some Christians know many verses of Scripture by heart and yet they fail to live according to them. The church is strong when she lives by her understanding.

Love changes the way you handle every life situation. If somebody offends you, love emboldens you to not respond to the offense but to forgive the offender and let Jesus respond instead of you. I encourage you to ask yourself regularly, "Do I behave like Christ?" It doesn't matter if you are a pastor, a leader, or a layman. It doesn't matter how many years or months you have been following Christ. What matters is whether your character and life reflect Jesus Christ or not. Only people who embody the nature of Jesus have the right to call themselves *Christians*, a word that originally meant "little Christs."

If Jesus's followers embody the nature of their King, there will be no need to prove that we are Christians. Our love and our works will convince people better than a thousand sermons. As Paul wrote:

> But we all, with unveiled face, beholding as in a mirror the glory of the Lord, are being transformed into the same image from glory to glory, just as by the Spirit of the Lord.
>
> **—2 Corinthians 3:18, NKJV**

As we shift, we need to realize that without being identified with God, without becoming kingdom minded, we will not change anything in our world. New seasons bring new assignments. National transformation is today's assignment. Only those who are increasingly filled with God's nature will become deliverers and saviors of their nation, community, and family.

Love people! Love them no matter who they are or what they do. Love people regardless of their faults. Love them unconditionally. God's love draws people, but our attitude often pushes them away. But if there is love, then that love draws and keeps them. Love is the strongest bonding agent in the universe. Love preserves people in the kingdom of God. If they do something wrong, love them. Even if you do not like socializing with them, continue to love them!

Love and help people before you ever try to influence them. Love them before they listen to you. Love them while delivering them from slavery. Love them while bringing them out of the world. Today, many ministers can teach, but fewer can love. That's why many churches remain so small and irrelevant. Some ministers think that as long as they teach somebody, everything else will fall into place. But nobody will listen to ministers of God if they don't love. People don't come to church to be taught. They're seeking love, and that's our first commission.

God's love doesn't permit us to hate anybody. It doesn't permit us to be bitter, angry, or hateful. Love for the land and its people will lead us to impact our nations. Let us be kingdom minded. Let us embody the nature of our King. Then let us go forth to rule in our promised lands.

KINGDOM PRINCIPLES

FROM CHAPTER 4

1. When Christians make church the focal point of their lives and ministry, they burn each other like an over-salted dish and blind each other like a room full of spotlights.

2. When a church loses focus, people get busy fighting among themselves. When our focus is not on finding our promised land and changing our society from right where we are, we start using kingdom resources to build our own kingdom.

3. There is absolutely no use in having a big church without changing culture, speaking to society, and curing social ills.

4. Egocentricism kills leadership because it shrinks their ambitions to the size of their own desires.

5. The gospel of salvation, in isolation, will not change the earth. When you teach a half-truth, you destroy the truth.

6. This world can only be properly managed by people who rule from a superior place and superior principles.

7. We must work better and harder than anybody else. The kingdom of God will work for us at the same level we are committed to the kingdom.

8. Only those who are increasingly filled with God's nature will become deliverers and saviors of their nation, community, and family. Love and help people before you ever try to influence them.

Chapter 5

HARD WORK
LEADS TO SUCCESS

Success in God's kingdom does not come just by finding your promised land, educating yourself, and becoming kingdom minded. It comes by putting those principles into practice with great effort and diligence. One of the most neglected ingredients in many Christians' lives is plain hard work. There is no shortcut around it. I am convinced that hard work is the missing element in many people's lives and that many spheres of society today are suffering at the hands of the devil because righteous people have not learned to work hard.

Hard work can create an unlikely ambassador. Hard work is the wealth of the poor man. Most anyone can work hard, and God will honor His principles by expanding the territory of hard-working people. Remember that God has exalted His principles above His name. He will not violate His principles. We can't just pray a prayer and expect Him to expand our borders. We can't just find our promised land and say, "Here I am, God. Bless me." He has given us strength to conquer that land ourselves through hard work.

I am one example of how hard work turned a nobody into a somebody. I had to learn to work hard at an early age as a matter of survival. To this day I believe I am perhaps the most unlikely person to help lead a nationwide revolution in a former Soviet republic. Yet God is using me to disciple a nation, and I am believing Him for much more. How did it happen? I believe it was partly because I learned hard work through very unfortunate circumstances. It became my ladder out of a life of kingdom irrelevance.

Without Father or Mother

Unlike most people reading this book, I grew up with no possessions and little opportunity. I never had real parents. I was born to a mother who chose not to raise me and a father I never knew. He was run out of our village before I was even born because people said he was too violent. I never even knew his name.

I grew up among forty small huts in the Nigerian village of Idomila, Ijebu-ode, Ogun State. My grandmother raised me, and I grew up believing she was my mother. My biological mother visited occasionally with her new husband and children, but I thought she was my aunt. I took the last name of my mother's family: Adelaja.

The Adelajas were a family of kings. My grandfather had been the king of our village, and two of my older uncles and one aunt served in powerful positions in Nigeria. My uncle was a leading figure in the Nigerian Institute of Foreign Affairs. My other uncle was secretary to the minister of economics. My aunt was a business tycoon, one of richest women in the country. My family was Presbyterian, but we did not really know God.

While I was growing up, my two uncles and aunt gave our family financial stability and enhanced our reputation among the people. In developing countries, families often depend on a few successful people to sustain them. We were not rich, but our basic needs were met, and my cousins and I had enough money to attend school.

But when I was six years old, a great tragedy befell us. Those three family pillars died mysteriously within six months of each other. The coincidence was so strange that a major newspaper ran a front-page story asking, "Was it a tragedy, or a curse?" Many people believed witchcraft played a role in the deaths.

The effect on my family was devastating. Our reputation and our finances plummeted. We were left without leaders. My grandmother, whom I believed was my mother, could hardly cope with the shock of losing three of her children. She went into a coma for an entire year.

I was six years old and had no way to survive. I had no food. I was the only member of my family left in the village with my grandmother, who was now incapacitated with grief. I had no choice but to start working to support myself. I went into the bush and cut down trees with an ax, tied the wood into bundles, and took it on my head to the nearest city to sell for firewood. I used the money to buy food and pay my school bills so I could keep learning.

When my grandmother got well, she joined me in chopping and selling firewood. She also taught me to make a cereal from corn pulp. It was like a breakfast custard. I had three jobs when I was just eight years old: harvesting firewood, making custard, and going house to house saying, "Who wants to buy custard? Who wants to buy firewood?" I kept attending school at St. Paul's Anglican Primary School, knowing somehow that education would provide a better future for me. I had to walk several kilometers barefoot to the city to sell my products and several kilometers more to the school in the nearby village.

As I grew into an adolescent, I became ashamed and self-conscious of my jobs. It was humiliating to walk the streets hawking wood and custard, but I had to. There was no other way. Then an even worse thing happened. When I was fifteen, my grandmother died, and I was left virtually alone. I had to fend for myself, so I rented farmland and began farming cassava, a type of yam. I needed the additional income to finish high school. I needed to buy my uniform, pencils, and other supplies, and the money I made selling firewood and custard was not enough. So I cleared and cultivated the land and grew cassava. People in the village would point me out to their children and say, "He is alone, but he is making a living for himself." I was a good example to them, but I was angry about my life. I thought there was no God or that He was wicked.

I had older uncles whom I considered brothers. One had gotten a scholarship and gone to Moscow to study. He urged me to do the same. He wrote me a letter that said, "The only hope you have in Nigeria is to get a scholarship. If you don't finish high school, you will live forever in that village." Scholarships were few, and thousands of people applied. But I took his advice and redoubled my efforts to do well in school. I was getting some financial help from my other aunt, whom I considered my sister. She had boyfriends that gave her access to money she shared with her brothers and me. But when I was eighteen, she came by one day and said she couldn't send me support anymore. "I got saved, and I can't have boyfriends again," she told me. I felt like my world had come to an end. I had no concept of being saved or living right. I was living like an unbeliever. I went to church but also to discos. Now my one extra source of money was cut off.

I managed to finish high school. I was not the top student, but I was good enough to have a shot at a scholarship. At age eighteen I left my village to work in a polyester factory in a bigger village. There I lived with an older relative and applied for a university scholarship. There was a lag time between when I applied and when I would find out if I received a scholarship. I worked all day in the factory, and I liked to come home and relax by watching the news on television. One day a religious program came on after the news. The preacher caught my attention because he was a dean of mathematics at a Nigerian university. For the first time I considered the gospel message. I became convinced it was true. I wanted God's forgiveness, so I went into my room and repented of my sins. It felt like two hundred kilograms of weight dropped from my shoulders. I went to the street immediately and felt like greeting everyone. I was determined to go to the end of the world and tell people that God is real.

I began to work even harder after giving my life to Jesus. Instead of just working my way out of poverty, I was now working for an eternal kingdom. Hallelujah! I could not believe the riches I had found. The gospel completely changed my mind and renewed my efforts. I became serious, ambitious, and determined to succeed in life. I stopped spending my time partying or running after girls. Soon the result of my application came: I had passed my school examinations and won a scholarship to study journalism in the Soviet Union. Six months after I met the Lord, I left the shores of Nigeria and headed for the heart of the communist empire. I was so new in Christ that I had never even belonged to a church.

THE BLESSING OF WORK

Hard work and the favor of the Lord rescued me from a life of oblivion. But many believers have wrong ideas about work. They think it's a curse, an obligation, a means of supporting themselves, or a means of getting rich. Even worse, some see work as entirely separate from their kingdom life. They think that working for God and advancing their own career are two different things. But God has established work as a blessing for mankind and for His kingdom. Work was part of Adam's calling before the Fall. His job was to subdue the earth, tend the garden, and manage the animals. For us, hard work is a key to subduing our own promised lands.

God Himself works, and so did Jesus:

> But Jesus answered them, "My Father has been working until now, and I have been working."
>
> —John 5:17, NKJV

Jesus worked, and works still, because work was established by His Father as something good for humanity. During His earthly life, Jesus worked as a carpenter and as a preacher. He fully devoted Himself to the ministry and showed a strong work ethic. Anyone who does not work disgraces himself and steals from the wealth of those who do labor.

> He who is slothful in his work
> Is a brother to him who is a great destroyer.
>
> **—Proverbs 18:9, NKJV**

If a man does not work, he gives nothing of value to the world. He is a thief. He is useless to God. We are made to bless each other through our labor. Work is good! You will not fulfill your potential in God's kingdom without hard work. Failure in life never means a person lacks gifts. But it may mean he failed to put the gifts to work. God gives everyone a chance to become successful. The resources you need to impose the kingdom on your sphere of influence are inside of you. Each person will give an account before God of how he used these talents and how much of his potential he fulfilled.

Some people don't work because they can't find a job that will pay them what they want. Some don't want to get a job for which they are "overqualified." But God will not give you something big if He doesn't see your faithfulness in small things. That low-paying job may be your first step toward discovering and ruling your promised land.

Some Christians have amazing talents but experience little results because they have not learned to work. Others are nothing but dreamers. They sit and wait for a breakthrough to come. But they forget that success won't drop into their laps like manna from heaven. People who think that God will do everything Himself while they just sit around and make big plans are pitiful.

A few years ago our church started a new system of home

groups called the System of Twelves. We appointed leaders of each group. But instead of actively seeking members, many leaders waited for twelve people to show up to their meetings. When just one person showed up, they came back to us and said, "This System of Twelves is ineffective. Nobody came!" But they hadn't added the key ingredient: hard work.

Work has many side benefits.

- It gives us money to pay for our basic needs.

- It keeps us mentally healthy by focusing our minds on something productive.

- It keeps us out of trouble.

- It reveals our gifts and helps us discover our potential and abilities. Work is the gift of God to man for him to discover himself.

- It is the means by which dreams, ideas, and goals become reality.

- It allows us to become a cocreator with God.

- It makes us a blessing to other people.

- It increases our skills and abilities.

But by far the most important aspect of work is that it allows us to exercise dominion over all of God's creation. As kings and priests of the earth, we are to do more work and be more diligent than anyone else.

> Whatever your hand finds to do, do it with your might; for there is no work or device or knowledge or wisdom in the grave where you are going.
> —**Ecclesiastes 9:10, NKJV**

> He who tills his land will be satisfied with bread,
> But he who follows frivolity is devoid of understanding.
> —**Proverbs 12:11, NKJV**

Only those who know how to work hard will be satisfied with results. God is not obliged to bless people who don't work hard. But he that tills his land will be satisfied with bread.

It's time to start working hard for the kingdom. I believe I would still be in that village in Nigeria had I not been forced to work hard. Part of God's favor to me was teaching me that lesson. Let's all work hard to develop our gifts, passions, and callings so we might have maximum impact for Christ. Hard work is necessary to develop the nature and character of Christ in ourselves. And hard work is absolutely critical to successfully bring the principles of God into our spheres of influence and in turn into the life of a nation. Remember how much hard work and battle Israel went through to enter its Promised Land. Let's train ourselves in this key kingdom principle so the land can become ours for the glory of God.

KINGDOM PRINCIPLES
FROM CHAPTER 5

1. Hard work is the wealth of a poor man.

2. Hard work is one if the missing elements in many Christians' efforts.

3. God has established work as a blessing for mankind and for His kingdom.

4. Hard work is a key to subduing your own promised land.

5. Jesus worked, and works still, because work was established by His Father as something good for humanity.

6. By far the most important aspect of work is that it allows us to exercise dominion over all of God's creation.

7. God is not obligated to bless people who don't work.

Chapter 6

THRIVING IN
PERSECUTION

O NCE WE SHIFT, IT IS NOT ALWAYS PLEASANT business. Often it involves suffering persecution. But that persecution is never without purpose.

The scholarship I received for a university education sent me to the Soviet Union. This was not my first choice. I wanted to go to the United States or Great Britain. I had heard much about the States as a superpower and the United Kingdom as another great modern place, and I wanted to see those worlds for myself. But the application board sent me to Russia. That country wanted to train people in developing countries like Nigeria so they would return to their countries and lead communist revolutions. I was a little wary of going there, but I sensed God had a purpose in it. Before I went to Russia a pastor in Nigeria told me, "It will be difficult, but if you survive it, you'll make it anywhere."

I left Nigeria in 1986, not realizing that I was about to get two educations: one at the Russian university, the other in the school of persecution. There I learned that a key to ruling my promised land is to enjoy the school of persecution. If you're not enrolled yet, you will be! I've been enrolled for years, and I doubt that I'll ever graduate. But guess what? I'm glad for persecution. Persecution has kingdom purposes. I'll explain why.

GOD SPEAKS TO YOU IN TIMES OF PERSECUTION

When I got to Russia I quickly became frustrated and disappointed. I was expecting Russia to be an economic superpower like America, not just a military superpower. I was shocked at the low standard of living and the poor economy. Worst of all, there was no church on Sundays. There was, in effect, no Sunday, just a weekend. There was no place to learn about God. As a new Christian I felt cut off from the teaching I needed. I cried and prayed, "God, why did You allow me to come to this place?" I tried to assemble the Nigerian students for prayer, but within weeks I was sent to Belarus to attend university there. I met a group of four African people who were involved in the underground church. To them I expressed my frustration over being in the Soviet Union, and one of them challenged me. "Why are you so frustrated? Why are you complaining? Ask God why He allowed you to come here. He must have a purpose." I had sensed that before, so I began to pray every day when I woke up and when I went to bed. I did that for two weeks. Then something supernatural happened to me that remains unique in all my experiences.

I went to bed one night, and while I slept Jesus came to me

and showed me my future. I saw myself preaching to a huge audience of white people. I was seeing miracles and signs and wonders happen. The next night the same thing happened, and again on the third night. I saw everything so clearly. I remember the clothes I wore. I was on stage with famous preachers. Then Jesus came, took the microphone from one of them, and gave it to me. The preacher stepped back, and I came forward. Jesus stood beside me. Miracles began to happen. I was calling out sicknesses. People were getting out of wheelchairs. People were coming to testify. When I woke up after the third night I was shocked. My three roommates were asleep, but I was so full from the realness of the experience that I could hardly believe they had slept through it. I felt a strong urge to open the Bible, and it seemed to open itself to Isaiah 61. The very first verse reads, "The Spirit of the Sovereign LORD is upon me." I read it over and over, and each time it was like hearing thousands of voices in my ears, veins, and cells, as if the whole room was full of voices shouting, "The Spirit of the Sovereign LORD is upon me, because the LORD has anointed me to preach good news to the poor!" It was like a tide of water filling me. Again I wondered why nobody else was waking up. Tears streamed from my eyes.

I had never preached before and was only a young convert, six months in the Lord. With those thoughts in my mind, I again opened the Bible, and it fell to Jeremiah 1.

"Do not say, 'I am only a child.' You must go to everyone I send you to and say whatever I command you. Do not be afraid of them, for I am with you and will rescue you," declares the LORD. Then the LORD reached out his hand and touched my mouth and said to me, "Now, I have put my words in your mouth. See, today I appoint you over

nations and kingdoms to uproot and tear down, to destroy
and overthrow, to build and to plant."

—Jeremiah 1:7–10

I closed the Bible to pray again, then felt like opening it again
to Habakkuk 2:

I will stand at my watch
and station myself on the ramparts;
I will look to see what he will say to me,
and what answer I am to give to this complaint.
Then the LORD replied:
"Write down the revelation
and make it plain on tablets
so that a herald may run with it.
For the revelation awaits an appointed time;
it speaks of the end
and will not prove false.
Though it linger, wait for it;
it will certainly come and will not delay."

—Habakkuk 2:1–3

In obedience I took my pen and wrote down my whole experience. When it was over I was mesmerized and perplexed. I had to
talk to someone, but I had to wait until after classes ended. Later
that day I caught up with my friend in the underground church to
tell him what had happened to me. He brought down a notebook
from his shelf and said that at 2:00 a.m. God had awakened him
to write down this message for a member of the fellowship. It was
confirmation of my dreams.

From that point on God's visions went silent. I never had

that kind of encounter again in my life. I studied in the Soviet Union for six years. During that time the Christians I knew went through many trials. Some were sent to psychiatric wards, others were dismissed from the university, and some were deported. Those of us who remained worshiped together in silence. While I was in my room with my roommate I would pretend to sleep so I could pray under my blanket. I had morning devotions in the bathroom. I often was convinced I too would be found out and deported.

One time in my first year there, my fellow students heard about my religious interest and warned me to hide my Bible in the bottom of my suitcase and not take it out until I got back to Nigeria six years later. "God does not exist here," they said. But I didn't hide it. I had even put a picture of Jesus over my bed. One evening after classes I heard banging on my door. I opened it and saw four men and a woman, our dean, my roommate, a KGB officer, and a communist party official. They pointed to the portrait of Jesus and said, "What is this?"

I said, "This isn't a *what*. It's a *who*."

"Remove it, or you'll be punished," they said. "Religious propaganda is punishable by law. You could go to prison under article 35."

I understood then that my roommate had been writing a secret dossier on me. I had been betrayed. I was frustrated and angry, but I heard God say in that moment, "This is only a picture. Remove it from the wall, but don't allow them to remove Him from your heart." So I removed it from the wall, but I continued to grow in the knowledge of Christ during my time in Belarus.

God trained me during the persecution. He taught me to rely on Him. He taught me to be wise in how I conducted myself.

He gave me a vision of my future that has guided me ever since. I believe He will do the same for you in times of persecution.

In Persecution You Learn New Skills

Some people want to be released from hardship before they have acquired the skills God wants them to have. In my case, God knew He wanted me to minister in Ukraine, so I needed to learn the Russian language and culture. If I hadn't come to Russia and stuck it out through the tough times, I never would have learned Russian and would not have fulfilled the destiny God had for me in Ukraine.

Even though I was hiding out as a Christian and occasionally suffering hardship because of it, I used the time to gain new skills and knowledge. When I came to Russia, I didn't know a word of the language. We were immersed in it for nine months and then started studying together with students who spoke it fluently. I had to take notes, listen to lectures, read, and do my homework in Russian. It was difficult. But I believed that God would help me to achieve it if I put in the necessary study.

I used to spend six hours a day in the library after lectures. Other students, even the Christians, fell away from their studies and from their faith because of worldly temptations. But I buried myself in books and learning. I exercised myself in godliness and became one of the best students.

I graduated from the university with honors. Only a few other students obtained that distinction, and some of them had to do the exams again. I was the only one who graduated with honors without having to retake any tests.

The skills and language I learned during those years laid the foundation for what God asked me to do in Ukraine shortly thereafter.

KINGDOM NATURE GETS IN YOU

Persecution also reveals your character. It contrasts your selfish nature with the kingdom nature God wants to work into you. It then gives you opportunities to grow the character of Christ inside of you.

When I arrived in Moscow during the heart of the cold war in the 1980s, Russians hadn't seen many black people. I and the other Africans in our group of students were harassed. They called me "chocolate" and "monkey." A Russian asked me once, "When you arrived in Moscow did they cut your tail off and give you clothes?" Some Africans got annoyed at insults like this and wanted to fight people, but for some reason I never got annoyed. When people stared at me or called me "monkey," I was happy that I was giving someone joy.

How are we supposed to respond to persecution? What should our reaction be? Our first reaction should always be joy and thanksgiving.

> Blessed are you when they revile and persecute you,
> and say all kinds of evil against you falsely for My sake.
> Rejoice and be exceedingly glad, for great is your reward

in heaven, for so they persecuted the prophets who were
before you.

—**Matthew 5:11–12**, NKJV

We need to thank Him for the tests because they lift us to a
much higher level in God, bringing us closer to Him. Hardship
gives us strength and confidence. The Bible says:

Rejoice always…in everything give thanks; for this is the
will of God in Christ Jesus for you.

—**1 Thessalonians 5:16, 18**, NKJV

Persecution may be the fastest way to become kingdom minded.
It's like a pressure cooker that pushes out the old nature.

Our second reaction is well shown in the Bible:

But I say to you, love your enemies, bless those who curse
you, do good to those who hate you, and pray for those
who spitefully use you and persecute you.

—**Matthew 5:44**, NKJV

Every time we are persecuted we need to respond with God's
love. Persecution gives us the perfect platform to overcome evil
with good. In every bad situation we learn to see Satan's motives
behind a person's actions. The person has nothing to do with it.
The devil is the initiator of persecution. That's why the Bible says:

For we do not wrestle against flesh and blood, but against
principalities, against powers, against the rulers of the

darkness of this age, against spiritual hosts of wickedness in the heavenly places.

—**Ephesians 6:12, NKJV**

Persecution is God's invitation to have a right response. We need not be irritated or angry with people. We need to love our enemies, to bless them, and to pray for them.

Our third reaction is prayer for those who harm us. This connects us with God in the most powerful way possible. Jesus said:

> But love your enemies, do good to them, and lend to them without expecting to get anything back. Then your reward will be great, and you will be sons of the Most High, because he is kind to the ungrateful and wicked.
>
> —**Luke 6:35**

I am sure you have had ungrateful and wicked authorities in your life. Your job is to show them God's love and stand in the gap for them. Our church prays for the leaders of our country all the time, and in times of difficulty our prayers for them intensify.

Our fourth reaction is freedom from fear. Men cannot *make* us afraid.

> The fear of man brings a snare,
> But whoever trusts in the LORD shall be safe.
>
> —**Proverbs 29:25, NKJV**

We are free people. Galatians 5:13 says that we have been called to freedom. We are free because the Holy Spirit lives in us.

Fear has no part in being free. Rather, it is a snare that prevents us from moving forward. Fear makes us an easy bait for the devil. By accepting fear in our life we automatically allow it to rule over us. But fear is not one of God's qualities; it doesn't belong to us at all. Let's send it back to its owner.

> For though we walk in the flesh, we do not war according to the flesh. For the weapons of our warfare are not carnal but mighty in God for pulling down strongholds, casting down arguments and every high thing that exalts itself against the knowledge of God, bringing every thought into captivity to the obedience of Christ.
>
> —2 Corinthians 10:3–5, NKJV

Finally, we need to be faithful and let God judge our persecutor. If people don't receive you or the gospel, shake the dust off your shoes and hand them over to God. It's OK to withdraw once you've been faithful. For example, there are churches in Russia that I oversee, but the Russian government revoked my visa, so I can't travel there anymore. Rather than warring with Russia in the flesh, I simply withdraw for now. I have been faithful to my calling there. I was willing to go, and I tried to go, but they stopped me. My job is to keep on loving them and blessing them, but to hand them over to God. A time will come when I believe God will open the border again, and I will travel there freely. Until then, I hand them over to Him.

Fear of persecution has limited the church and hence the power of God to the four walls of our sanctuaries. We enjoy the comfort of it so much, we forget that Jesus left the comfort of heaven and sacrificed everything to bring His kingdom to us on Earth. Today

He is asking us to go to the world and endure all the world can throw at us. The earth will become ours if we will only act as Jesus did in Philippians 2:7–9.

> [He] made himself nothing,
> > taking the very nature of a servant,
> > being made in human likeness.
> And being found in appearance as a man,
> > he humbled himself
> > and became obedient to death—
> > even death on a cross!
> Therefore God exalted him to the highest place
> > and gave him the name that is above every name.

Persecution is part of the Christian lifestyle. Expect it, and rejoice in it as you grow into the stature of a mighty man or woman of God.

KINGDOM PRINCIPLES
FROM CHAPTER 6

1. A key to ruling your promised land is to enjoy the school of persecution.

2. Some people want to be released from hardship before they have acquired the skills God wants them to have.

3. Persecution reveals your character. It contrasts your selfish nature with the kingdom nature God wants to work in you.

4. Persecution gives us the perfect platform to overcome evil with good.

5. Persecution is God's invitation to have a right response.

6. Be faithful and let God judge your persecutor. It's OK to withdraw once you've been faithful.

7. Fear of persecution has limited the church and hence the power of God to the four walls of our sanctuaries.

Chapter 7

GO TO THE
LEAST OF THESE

O NE OF THE HARDEST LESSONS I EVER LEARNED about ruling my promised land is that God usually starts at the bottom of society, not the top. He loves to serve "the least of these" (Matt. 25:40), not the leaders. When Christ was born, the angels went to shepherds, not Caesar. Jesus ministered to the poor, not the well fed. If you really want to build the kingdom of God, start by serving the people who are considered the least important and least valuable around you.

When I completed my journalistic studies in Belarus, communism was just crumbling, and I and other Christians had begun taking the gospel message to the streets more boldly. It was an exciting time of new freedoms, but the old powers had not lost their sting. Because of my religious activities the government asked me to leave Belarus. I resisted strongly in prayer, but God said to me clearly and distinctly, "Leave Belarus." I protested, "No, Lord, this is my promised land. I cannot leave." I had sown my life there for seven years. Now it appeared that God wanted to send me back to Africa. Finally I gave up the fight. I decided that if the Lord wanted to use me in Africa, that was His decision. I was heartbroken but obedient.

But God didn't want to send me to Africa after all. Rather, He opened a new door for me to come to Ukraine. I got a call from a television station in Kyiv that needed a journalist who spoke Russian. My fianceé, Bose, a Nigerian student whom I had met in Russia, agreed to join me there. I started my journalism career in Kyiv, helping to produce and script shows for this pioneering television station. I was having much early success, but after only a year in Kyiv, I felt God nudging me to begin another church. I didn't want to go down that road again. Every time I started a work, God called me away from it. For three months I wrestled with God. Every time I prayed I heard the words, "You have to start a church." At last I asked Him, "Why do I need to start a church? Why is it so essential?" Then God told me something that set the foundation for my life ever since. He said, "Here in Ukraine I want to raise up strong, large churches with many thousands of members for the purpose of spreading the gospel throughout the whole world. In the same way the Soviet Union planted communism around the world, so I will use the nations of the former Soviet Union to take the good news everywhere."

I was dumbfounded, because the largest church in Ukraine at the time had only seven hundred people. But the Lord kept impressing on my heart that He wanted me to train reaper warriors to bring in the final harvest, especially in China and the nations of the Arab world. His glory would come to the land of Ukraine as He used the nation to help gather in the final harvest. He said I hadn't even started my ministry yet. This time He would not take me away from my church, as He did earlier. This church would be my home base for the ministry He called me for.

I had arrived in my promised land. This was what the Lord had been preparing me for. I felt certain that the destinies of many people depended on how I would respond to God.

I did not quit my journalism job at first, but I knew it was no longer my calling. Journalists always spread bad news. I was now called to spread the good news. My mind turned to the strategy I might use to accomplish the goal God had set before me of building a large church in Europe. I was only in my mid-twenties, but I made an announcement on television that anyone who wanted to study the Bible could come to my house, and I gave the address. I was hoping to attract professors and students from the local university. I envisioned having a church full of rich and powerful people who would get saved and do great things for God.

I was disappointed when one of the first people to arrive was Natasha, an alcoholic. She was captivated by the message of the gospel, though at first she understood little of it. She simply felt joy being with us. The handful of others who showed up the first time were also simple people with alcohol and drug problems. They looked old and dejected. This happened again the next week, and the next. Nobody came but a handful of derelicts. I redoubled my efforts and stood on street corners handing out invitations to "normal" people. It was strange for a black man to stand on the street corner inviting people to church. Nobody responded.

I became more and more disillusioned. I didn't even know what to do with the few down-and-outers who came to services.

Finally I went home and prayed, "God, You told me I would build a megachurch for You. Why is nobody coming?" I decided not to sleep that night until I had an answer. At 3:00 a.m. God led me to Mark 12:37, which says that "the common people heard him gladly" (KJV). That sentence pierced my heart like a burning shaft. I realized that God had sent His friends to me and I was turning up my nose at them.

God began to minister to me and said, "Many people think that serving Me means preaching from the pulpit. That is not My understanding of ministry. Preaching and church ministries are just tools and instruments you can use. But ministry is really about touching people. Get rid of your tie and jacket. Go out of your pulpit. Ministry is not about putting on your suit and handing out invitations and advertisements and expecting people to come hear you at church. Who are you, especially in this society? You are expecting people to go out of their way to come listen to you. They will never do it. If you were one of them, you wouldn't cross the street to listen to a Nigerian pastor, either. How do you expect them to do that? You're not playing basketball or something else they want to see. And you want them to let you teach them how to live right? Yes, there is prejudice in this society, but that's not the only problem. You are part of the problem. Your understanding of church ministry is faulty."

I was weeping. God's message to me continued, "Take those ideas of ministry out of your mind. If you want to serve Me, be like Me. The ordinary people, the outcast, the poor, the down and out, the drunkards all felt welcomed by Me. That's why I said I was naked and nobody clothed Me. That is ministry to Me. If you can take care of them, you will take care of Me. If you love them like I love them, you will love Me. If I can trust you with them, then in the years to come I will also be able to trust you with ordinary people and the elite, powerful, strong, and wealthy. But if I can't trust you with the naked and hungry, I won't be able to trust you with anybody."

My mind changed that night. All my life I had thought, "If I could only preach well and be eloquent and anointed, I would fulfill God's will." But God's revelation blew apart my conception of ministry. I saw that if I could make ordinary people feel good around me, I'd be like Jesus. I decided then to become trustworthy with the down-and-outers, the outcasts, the unloveables, and the untouchables.

BREAKTHROUGH

People ask me where my breakthrough in ministry started. It wasn't in learning and absorbing the Russian culture and language, though this gave me invaluable tools. It wasn't learning how to preach or feel comfortable ministering before a group. No. My breakthrough came when I left the pulpit and went to the streets to look for the outcasts.

Truthfully, I never even knew such people lived in Kyiv in any substantial numbers. I had always kept myself with university students and other so-called ordinary people. I didn't know there was a whole world of drunkards, drug addicts, and forgotten people living in the shadows of society.

But when I reached out to them, doors opened up wide for

ministry. Someone in our church knew of a hospital where drunkards were kept, so I began to go there and beg the doctors to give me one hour to be with the patients. I would bring along Natasha who testified how she was delivered from alcoholism, and then I prayed for the patients. There, my ministry began. God began to honor that sacrifice with supernatural anointing. When I prayed for drunkards and addicts they would suddenly wake up from their stupor. The power of God would descend on them so strongly that they would be set free in an instant. As a result they began to come to church. Then their mothers would come asking, "What did you do to my son? We spent everything to try to help him. We don't care if you're red, white, or black. You've given us back our son." In one year the church grew to a thousand people, and it added a thousand people every year after that. We changed meeting places six times in one year, going from east to west to south to north of the city. But it didn't matter anymore. I knew I had the key. If I could love people with this love, I could change the world.

In the third year of our existence, the outcasts began to look respectable. They were getting jobs and homes, and nobody could tell they had been drunkards and drug addicts before. People thought they were normal, and so normal people starting coming to our church too. Wealthy people joined us, as did the influential and the politicians. Many of them would invite friends without mentioning that I was a black pastor, because people wouldn't come if they knew in advance I was from Nigeria. In that society I was a monkey, a chocolate, even a chocolate bunny. But when people came and felt the Spirit of God, they looked past their prejudices, braved the rejection of their families, and made the kingdom their priority. In my first four years in Russia, I could not get any European saved, but now thousands were coming because our church was touching ordinary people.

To this day, serving the least of these is the primary concern of our church. It is our foundation. Is it yours? Take a moment to think, who are the "least of these" in your world? The janitors, gardeners, service people, cafeteria workers, secretaries around you? Jesus surrounds us in the form of other people. To reach new heights in the kingdom we must extend our hand to the depths and become a friend of the unwanted and unloved. There, God will begin to transform our character. If God can touch the down and outs of society through us, only then will He trust us with the rich and elite of our nation. That is exactly what happened in Ukraine.

God did what He promised, and now people think that we are a church of the rich and powerful. Various businesspeople are attracted to the church. We formed Club 1000, where we expect to have one thousand millionaires. So far over five hundred people have registered to be part of the club.

Now we have dozens of members in parliament on different levels in our church. We have parliament members on regional, city, and state levels. In the city of Kyiv the mayor is a member of our church. The Supreme Court chief justice is a member of our church. Also the church party controls 20 percent of the city parliament—that is the faithfulness of God. If God cannot trust you with the least, He cannot trust you with the greats of the society. We are no longer known as the church of the down and out.

KINGDOM PRINCIPLES
FROM CHAPTER 7

1. The destinies of many people depend on how you respond to God.

2. God loves to serve those who are considered least in a society.

3. Preaching and church ministries are just tools and instruments you can use, but ministry is really about touching people.

4. God won't entrust you with the greatest until He can trust you with the least.

5. My breakthrough came when I left the pulpit and went to the streets to look for the outcasts.

6. If you can love people with God's love, then you can change the world.

7. To reach new heights in the kingdom, you must extend your hand to the depths and become a friend of the unwanted and unloved.

Chapter 8

LEARN
TO FIGHT!

AFTER OUR MARCH ON CITY HALL, WHEN THE
mayor promised us property, we waited for his
word to be fulfilled. We waited to hear what piece
of property they had given us. We waited and waited. There
was only silence. Our church sent representatives back to city
hall to inquire about answers, but they were punted around
like footballs from one office to another. Soon we realized
we were being swept under the rug. We had no signatures,
no paperwork, only the mayor's verbal promise. The city
had solved its immediate problem—removing us from the
square—but it had no intention of following through on its
end of the bargain. We'd been duped.

This should not have surprised me. Our church had felt the opposition of the government and media of Ukraine before. Through it all we learned that we would have to fight many battles. (If you think nations are just going to fall into your hands, you're dreaming.) Everybody in the world is fighting for power. As kingdom people we are blessed with the tools that actually work, but it still will be a tough fight. Let me share principles that will help you win the fight.

WHEN BATTLE COMES

Our church endured its first barrage of criticism in 1997 when we had three thousand people. The government and media began to take notice of us because of our growing size. They didn't like what they saw—a threat to the national identity, a corrupter of Ukrainian culture, a potentially powerful force in society. They began accusing me of many things—trying to run for president, destroying tradition, corrupting people's minds, dealing drugs, making money through the church, selling alcohol, hypnotizing people, practicing black magic, being an agent of the CIA, and being a cult leader. Imagine being all those things at once! The accusations flew so thick that we couldn't have defended our name if we'd tried. We needed God.

The police seized my passport and revoked my official permission to preach as a foreigner. My visa mysteriously "got lost," and I was accused of being an illegal resident. They tried to prohibit me from preaching. At one point the government gave me two weeks to leave the country.

During the next several years, I battled twenty-two lawsuits.

I was still on television then, and Orthodox Christians would call and attack us on the air. They said, "We don't need black men to talk to us. Blacks only received Jesus two hundred years ago. We have been a Christian country for a thousand years."

Then the threats on my life began. On one occasion our ushers were given funeral wreaths and told, "Prepare your pastor for his funeral." When I received those wreaths, humanly speaking, I was scared, but God assured me from the first moment that it wouldn't amount to anything. I remained joyful and calm, as though everything were going just fine. In my mind, God had already dealt with the situation. The threat disappeared.

One day I received a letter warning me that my helpers and I were going to be victims of an act of reprisal. The letter said that people living in Ukraine would be far better off as drug addicts than as fanatics who believed in God. The letter was full of threats. I had already received several other similar letters from nationalists, gangsters, and drug dealers. These did cause me to worry and at one point became a huge burden for me. I declared a weeklong fast, asked the whole congregation to pray, and went to God to talk to Him. I said, "What's all this about? My ministry is Your responsibility. So why has this heavy weight come over me?"

God impressed on me just to keep on doing what He told me to do.

After that I was able to relax. Before long the organization that had threatened me got into their own difficulties. Nothing came of their threats.

One day a woman from our church had a vision of a man coming toward me pointing a gun. She started interceding for me fervently in the Spirit. At that particular moment I was in an underground subway station and there really was a man coming toward me with a gun. But when he was still a few yards away from me, the gun dropped out of his hand, and before he could pick it up again, I disappeared into the crowd.

On another occasion some people brought guns to a service where I was preaching. That night God showed three of our believers in advance, in the spiritual realm, who these people were and even where they were going to sit. The meeting proceeded because I had already taken appropriate measures, spiritually and physically, to stem the threat. Our church has its own guards, but this night we also requested that the military place some of its soldiers in the auditorium for the duration of our service. With my own eyes I saw these three individuals who wanted to murder me realize that they had no chance of doing so, so they got up and left. We never saw them again.

For the most part these attacks did not worry me. I slept as soundly as I ever have. But my wife was concerned that one day she'd hear that I'd been killed. She thought we could leave the country and go back to Nigeria. At least there we would be accepted, she said. We looked like everyone and nobody would notice us. But we never seriously considered moving back to Nigeria. Our promised land was in Ukraine.

GAINING VICTORY

There is no victory without battle. Battle is the normal state of affairs for the believer. This is a contested planet. The devil won't just walk away from hard-earned territory.

But God uses battle to train us. Psalm 105:19 says, "Until the time that his word came to pass, the word of the LORD tested him" (NKJV). Before the Word of God comes fully into your life, it will try you. It will test you. It will see what your reactions are to the battles. It will see if you are established in the Word and the revelation God has made available to you.

Before Abraham became father of nations God tried him. Jacob was tried by Laban when he wanted to marry Rachel. Jesus was tried in the desert before His ministry began.

Every blessing, just like a coin, has two sides. Often we think that God's blessings protect us from tests. Just the opposite is true. With each blessing come temptations, tests, and opposition. As soon as God makes you stronger and multiplies your power and influence, you might as well brace yourself for the next wave of tests and battles. Every victory, every success God gives will make others jealous, cause hatred, and invite opposition. The devil will find out about your blessing and will make sure that your blessing becomes your "headache." But the Bible says:

> And we know that all things work together for good to those who love God, to those who are the called according to His purpose.
>
> **—Romans 8:28, NKJV**

It's important to remember that we are attacked not because God dislikes us, but because the devil doesn't like God blessing us. This is especially true when you discover your promised land and make up your mind to have maximum impact in your sphere of influence. That's why the time of battle, like the time of persecution, is the time to thank and praise God. It's high time to see

God's blessing behind our struggles. It's time to get strengthened in faith and know that the blessings of God are stronger than the devil's attacks. Greater is He who is in us than he who is in the world (1 John 4:4).

If the devil starts putting obstacles in your way, that means God has a special plan of blessing for you. The devil's attacks are a proof of his powerlessness before us. If you realize this, it will be easier for you to fight the battles. There is no way to greatness without passing through trials by fire. Remember that as soon as Pharaoh saw that the Israelites were multiplying, the blessing turned to the other side of the coin. He began to persecute them. This is the normal sequence of events for God's people. Therefore when you are thrust into battle, don't complain, but remember that everything works together for good for those who love God.

Passing the Test of Battle

Some Christians fail the test of battle because they are timid. They claim they are being humble, but they are actually afraid to fight battles because they are not dead to their own ego. They are catering to their desire for self-preservation. They are not living totally for Him.

Every battle is a chance to give up. When I arrived in Ukraine, a preacher said to me, "You don't need to start a church here because nothing would ever come of it. Do you really think that people would ever come to a church led by you? You can't speak the language fluently, and you have a different skin color. You have no chance of being successful here."

In this preacher's opinion, there was a long list of problems obstructing my pathway to success. But I remembered Proverbs 30:24, which says:

> Four things on earth are small,
>   yet they are extremely wise:
> Ants are creatures of little strength,
>   yet they store up their food in the summer.
> **—Proverbs 30:24–25**

When I was a boy, I was curious about ants. I wondered what happened to them in winter and the rainy season in Africa where I grew up. I thought that they lived only in the summer and died from the cold, rain, and snow in winter. But when the next summer came and the ants emerged again, I wondered why the cold and snow couldn't destroy them. I learned that they survived because they had been wise and used the summer to store up their food provision for winter.

Ants are small, but they behave in big ways. Like the ant, I have many disadvantages in the circumstances I'm in. I'm dark-skinned in Ukraine, where there are few blacks. I have a strong African accent, and when I speak Russian it's hard sometimes for people to understand what language I'm speaking: Ukrainian, Russian, Byelorussian, or English. Once I walked up to a man at a bus stop and invited him to our church. Using a derogatory expletive, he retorted with hatred and disdain, "What do you want?" But did this stop me? No. I know that one day this man will repent of his response and understand that I wanted to help him.

Do I have a dark skin? Yes. Do I speak broken Russian? Yes. But the Holy Spirit lives in me. I have the Word of God, the Bible, in my hands. I have a brain that can think, eyes that can see, and a mind that can learn all that I need to know. The same applies to you. God does not put us into battles without the proper weapons. In fact, your best weapons may be your own "weaknesses." When people tell me, "You are emotional and have a hot temperament," I answer, "Yes, that's right. But I use these 'negatives' for good. What a pity that you are not as hot-tempered as me. I am going to use this temperament for preaching the gospel." This isn't just talk. God really does use it. Your weakness, in God's hands, becomes your strength. The ants are "creatures not strong," according to Scripture, but they are exceedingly wise. Be wise. Don't let size fool you.

When the Israelite spies saw the people living in the Promised Land, they were fooled by their size. They were mortified and called them giants (Num. 13). In the same way, there are "giants" on your way to ruling your promised land. There are problems, hardships, resistance, and persecution. Do not be afraid of them, because God Himself will fight for you. God will sometimes allow problems and hardships in our lives in order to strengthen our spirits and teach us to put our trust in the Maker instead of putting it in our own strength. What is required of us is courage and the spirit of a warrior. We must possess the characteristics of a conqueror to take possession of our land of Canaan.

Many believers wander in the wilderness instead of getting into their promised land. They are afraid of hardship and fail to put their trust in God. They know they should study, but fear or laziness overcomes them; they know they have to work hard in the ministry, but they have no desire to fight. The fruits of Canaan belong to those who fight, who put their trust in God, and who walk in obedience to Him.

"If you are willing and obedient,
You shall eat the good of the land;
But if you refuse and rebel,
You shall be devoured by the sword";
For the mouth of the LORD has spoken.
—Isaiah 1:19–20, NKJV

HOW BATTLES END

God's favor will often reconcile you with your enemies. Without understanding what is happening, those who sought your life will suddenly calm down and cease being at war with you.

That happened in my life. During the period of battle when our church fought against the government and media and shady organizations in society, the volleys of criticism came so fast and relentlessly that we couldn't even answer them all. I was personally disparaged, maligned, and threatened with savage punishment.

Then one day I had to meet with the leader of one of the nation's political groups. Everybody had warned me about how dangerous he was. His companions were extreme nationalists, leaving no doubt to how they would treat a dark-skinned man. But I knew the way God's favor and mercy work. When I met and greeted that man, he was taken by surprise. I seized that moment of his confusion and hugged him. We talked for two hours, and he accepted Jesus Christ as his Lord and Savior. He told me about the actions they had planned to take against me in the future, and his enmity melted away. Today he and I are no more on the opposite sides of the barricades, but one in the body of Christ.

The first result of battle is that your enemies become your friends.

The next result is flat-out victory. When the crescendo of outrage at our church reached a high pitch in society, the government dispatched a team of psychologists, doctors, and folk practitioners to observe our services. They wanted the experts to prove I was manipulating people. Instead, the team produced a certificate giving the church a clean bill of health. I took that certificate, framed it, and put it on the wall of my office. It's a war trophy!

Three years after the battle started I had won every lawsuit brought against me. I was not deported. The church did not shut down, as the government had hoped. In fact, we continued to grow in quality, quantity, and reputation. God sent influential politicians to our church, and fifty members of parliament pledged their support to me in a letter to the president and attorney general. Our period of greatest battle coincided with one of our periods of greatest growth.

That's the third result: you will reap positive benefits for a long time afterward. Not only did God enhance our reputation in the country because of all the discussions about us, but in the midst of battle we also started several practices that became crucial to our spiritual health in the future. The most important of these are the fasting and prayer retreats we started holding twice a year in 1997. They continue to this day. Twice a year, in July and December, I gather one to two thousand leaders for prayer and fasting for ten days. Believers are taught to wait upon God in prayer and fasting for an average of ten to twelve hours daily. As a church, we agree that these retreats form the backbone of all our efforts. They help us shift from church as usual to having an impact on Ukraine.

The fourth lesson about battles is this: there's always another one on the horizon. Our church still faces battles. Just a few months ago a member of Russia's parliament told the *Wall Street Journal* that our church is "an alien force that must be stopped." He said, "There is no question they [evangelical churches] are a tool of the U.S." He would like to see new laws limiting the activities of churches like ours.[1]

Another current battle involves Russia, which is unhappy with our church's influence on Ukrainian politics. Recently a new mayor was elected in Kyiv. He is an outspoken member of our church. This angered the Kremlin. Soon a prime-time Russian television talk show invited me to be their guest, but when I arrived in Moscow for taping, border guards at the airport told me my visa had been revoked. The program aired without me, and a panel of psychologists and lawmakers accused me of zombifying people and illegally practicing medicine.

Am I worried about this? No. The bad publicity only raises our profile in the region, and anyway, it's too late for Russia to stop me. I will outlast them, and one day my visa will be restored.

When our church faces major challenges, I always pray that the Lord would not shorten our battle but teach us how to fight. If you haven't yet attained the result you want in battle, then pray for the pressure to continue until you have learned what to do.

After marching on city hall we realized that our church was being ignored and that we wouldn't get land to build on after all. In spite of our growing stature in Ukraine, the government still did not consider us a force to be reckoned with. We found ourselves at another crossroads. Would we allow the government to ignore us and go back to the way things were? Or would we take to the

111

streets again? We decided that we must honor God's word to us. We would disobey again and return to the streets in protest. We would fight the new battle and show them that the people of a country cannot be ignored.

This time we would march in much greater numbers. The lesson had been learned: to do nothing is to come to nothing. God was not answering my prayers to miraculously resolve our sanctuary problem. Instead He was taking us on a journey to bring permanent change to our corner of the planet.

KINGDOM PRINCIPLES
FROM CHAPTER 8

1. Battle is normal as you move into your promised land. It means God is going to bless you if you persevere and stand your ground.

2. There is no victory without battle. The devil won't just walk away from hard-earned territory.

3. God uses battle to train us.

4. With each blessing come tempations, tests, and opposition.

5. It's important to remember that we are attacked not because God dislikes us but because the devil doesn't like God blessing us.

6. God does not put us in battles without the proper weapons.

7. God will sometimes allow problems and hardships in our lives in order to strengthen our spirits and teach us to put our trust in the Maker instead of putting it in our own strength.

Chapter 9

YOU ARE A
DELIVERER

O
N Friday, April 2, 2004, our congregation
marched for a second time on city hall, and this
time we were twenty thousand people strong—
six times the size of our original group. We were bigger. We
were bolder. We were more unified. And we were not going
home until the government lived up to its original promise.

Our march was highly organized. Everyone belonged to a group
of five. We carried flags of our country. Our choir members wore
their blue robes and shook pom-poms. We held hands and sang and
praised our way to the city center. It was almost like one of our
lively church services, only in the middle of the city. I'm quite sure
people had never seen anything like it. At city hall we assembled,
and I spoke to the media and said, "As believers, if we don't make
the authorities stick to their promises, nobody else will. We should

display the civil norms for people to know there should be decency in everything. Let our yes be yes and our no be no. People can't go on like this with no electricity in the complex we're gathering in. The toilets are closed; people aren't allowed inside. There is a huge army of people. We're Ukrainians, citizens of this country. We have rights. We say, let us build the building ourselves, but please give us the opportunity."

Bold words stirred in my spirit. I knew what I was thinking hit the nerves of our society, yet I could never have imagined this statement would become famous throughout our nation. I said to political leaders, "If you will not accept responsibility for this country, then I will!"

We chanted our slogans with power and joy, saying, "Dear mayor! The people are waiting for you!" But from city hall there was only silence. Nobody came out, so we warmed up in a familiar manner, by praising and dancing. The police were shocked. Our message was not hatred and rebellion but love. We proclaimed that God loved Ukraine, and we, God's kingdom people, were taking responsibility for our rights and for the ills of the country. Our balloons, banners, and flags were of many colors, foreshadowing the orange-themed revolution that was to come. People linked arms and twirled. For some onlookers it must have looked like the wildest religious service they'd ever seen.

After four hours we got our breakthrough. The assistant to the mayor came out and spoke to us through his megaphone. "I spoke on the phone with the mayor," he said. "He is busy now with regular meetings. But this matter will be settled this month, and the land will be set aside."

This was encouraging, but we knew better than to go home yet.

We refused to disband and instead prayed and sang and celebrated until the mayor himself came out and spoke with us. This time we made sure to get his signature, not just his promise. The city told us immediately what land it was giving us—a well-situated 6.2-acre plot that would accommodate us.

Then I got on a megaphone and said to the twenty thousand people, "We have documents—signed documents. Congratulations." The people chanted "thank you" to the city building. That day the city council kept their word. Our victory was finally sealed.

I learned a major lesson that day. It's not enough to have large numbers or justice on your side. God needs deliverers like Moses to rise up and lead people to victory, using wisdom and power. Earthly authorities respect only visible and tangible force. They will not give in easily. The government of the city was able to ignore our request and trick us into going home after our first march. But when they saw tens of thousands of people on the streets, they felt outmatched and had to give in.

To rule your promised land you cannot rely on the goodwill of leaders. You must exert your power, become a godly leader, and actively take the land. We must all become Moseses.

Let's look at five things Moses did to free his nation.

1. Moses identified with his nation.

To be a deliverer you must identify with your nation. You need to believe that God cares for your nation as a whole. And you need to see yourself as an integral part of your nation.

Too many Christians see themselves as existing apart from their nation. They say they are citizens of heaven. That is true to a point, but it does not let us off the hook for completing our work here on Earth. It is impossible to be separate from your nation. God does not see you as an isolated individual with no connection to the society around you. Extreme individualism does not work in the kingdom of God. You are part of your nation and are responsible for its sins or its righteousness. You are also part of your family and workplace and local body of believers. This is an inescapable part of being human. The way to be effective for the kingdom is to identify with your nation, family, employer, and local community. Take responsibility for them and use your strength and all your skills to bring kingdom principles.

In Jeremiah 29:7 the Lord spoke to people living among unbelieving nations. He expressly gave them responsibility for the nation in which they lived, even though that nation was not their own by birth.

> And seek the peace of the city where I have caused you to be carried away captive, and pray to the LORD for it; for in its peace you will have peace.
>
> —NKJV

In other words, don't try to excuse yourself from working for the good of your nation, because God has linked your peace with its peace. There are no exceptions for believers who are trying to follow God over in their own little corner. No, it's your job to make sure peace and prosperity come. Fix the economy. Fix the political problems. Fix the ungodliness in entertainment and sports and business. God is expecting it of you. He identifies you with your nation. Until you see this, you will miss the heart of God.

Why doesn't God let us identify only with ourselves or with other believers? Because "God so loved the world." He is still trying to redeem the planet, not just tend to the redeemed. Remember that the Good Shepherd left the ninety-nine to rescue the one. Jesus came to give the entire world light. He identified so fully with us that He died a human death. He took personal responsibility for the darkness of the earth. But He didn't stop there. He passed the light-bearing task over to us. As long as He was in the world, He was its light. But now we are the light of the world.

Moses understood this valuable key. He told the people of Israel, "I neither ate bread nor drank water, because of all your sin which you committed in doing wickedly in the sight of the LORD, to provoke Him to anger" (Deut. 9:18, NKJV). Moses was willing to suffer for the sins of his nation. True deliverers identify themselves with their nation or group. They are willing to take the blame upon themselves. We too must learn to stand before God for our nation, just as we stand before Him for our personal needs.

Moses was even willing to give up the comforts of Pharaoh's palace, where he was raised, to identify himself with Israel, which was a people in slavery. We must also identify ourselves with our nation so that we forget about our own lives. This strong identification will give us strength to stand for our nation until our last breath and last drop of blood. Often we say that we love our nation, but do we really? Many Christians try to love their nation from afar, as if it is something not to be embraced or touched. But true identification gets mud on our hands. It makes us part of the problem and the solution. It turns us into radical, passionate people of action. Once your life is on the line with the success or failure of your nation, you can no longer be complacent. You will be compelled to innovate and improve and stand against principles of darkness. You will see the affairs of your nation and family and workplace as very much your business. You will see that it's in your best interests to give your life to promote kingdom principles so your nation is transformed for God's glory.

I used to see myself as a pastor in Ukraine. But I have changed my job description. I am now the deliverer of a nation. I have identified myself with Ukraine. Her peace is my peace. Her success is my success. Her sins are my sins. Her failures are my failures. And I will share in her salvation too as we transform our country into a model of kingdom principles. You cannot rule your promised land from the sidelines. You can't phone it in. You must identify yourself with your nation as Moses did.

2. Moses spoke for God.

It's not enough to hide God's Word in your heart. You must speak for God in your place of influence. If you don't represent and promote kingdom principles, you are harming your nation, family, employer, or group by denying them the answer. God has placed you there to be His spokesperson.

Moses did not initially want to be the spokesman for God and for the nation of Israel, but he accepted his calling. You too are a Moses, even if you don't want to be. Everyone on Earth is called to be a deliverer in their sphere of authority or expertise. It's not optional. As a child of God you belong to an army of deliverers who lead from a million positions of authority throughout society.

How do you speak for God at work? By promoting kingdom principles wherever you can. You stand up for integrity, justice, patience, honesty, respect, and compassion. You might deliver your employer from corruption by refusing to pad expense accounts or under-report profits. You might influence your company to help the needy through a new compassion program.

Every decision you make either delivers or enslaves people. There are a million ways to establish the kingdom of God one choice at a time. Every decision is founded either in righteousness or unrighteousness. Every choice can be a building block of national reformation. It is not enough to see our everyday choices as mere private decisions in our personal walk with God or our career. No, they affect everyone around us, and ultimately they shape our lives and society.

The more you speak for God, the more God moves into areas where darkness used to rule. Christians are the most valuable citizens of any country or corporation because in every circumstance we take God's side. Believers change the atmosphere and direction of society wherever we go, whether at a board meeting, church, or the PTA. What is your current sphere of influence? How are you speaking for God there? Be a Moses, and speak boldly for God.

3. Moses confronted Pharaoh.

Sometimes speaking for God means confronting powerful rulers as Moses did. Ungodly leaders can be stubborn. If Moses had relied on the goodwill of Pharaoh, the people of Israel might still be in Egypt. That's why there are times when you will be called upon not just to add your voice to the national conversation but also to confront a person or group of people who are acting unrighteously, just as my church confronted the government by marching on city hall.

Pharaoh is a symbol of anything or anyone who keeps people from serving God. Remember that God's request through Moses was, "Let My people go, that they may hold a feast to Me in the wilderness" (Exod. 5:1, NKJV). As Moseses, you and I confront people and powers that keep people from worshiping and serving God. Psalm 86:9 says, "All nations...shall come and worship before You" (NKJV). That is a dream in the heart of God, and we must bring that dream to pass. No Pharaoh can stand in the way.

By confronting unrighteous leaders, you are doing them and your nation a favor. If you don't boldly bring kingdom principles into society, you undermine your leaders' ability to act in righteousness. How are they to know the right way if you don't tell them? They must feel the pressure, knowing that people in their nation are standing for truth and justice. Then they will act righteously, even if it's not from a pure motive. But as they feel that pressure, God has a chance to change their hearts.

Our church's representatives experienced this firsthand during a meeting with the then-mayor of Kyiv some years ago. He was making a decision that affected our church in important ways. While other believers from our church were praying elsewhere, God was doing His part by changing this man's heart right before their eyes. Instead of the normal hostility they received at city hall, they felt the atmosphere was pleasant, almost welcoming. They could feel God's presence where they used to get refusals. The mayor said that soon he would come to God too. That day our church saw that the heart of the king is in the hand of the Lord, as the Bible tells us in Proverbs 21:1.

If each one of us manifests God in our area of society, it gives room for God to touch people's hearts, including the hearts of executives and rulers. If the people reveal God, He will change the heart of the king of that country; He will soften the hearts and turn them toward the care of the people. God can fill the heart of a king with love for His people. When people do God's will, the heart of the king belongs not only to God but also to the people of the country.

You may think, "I'm just a worker," or "I'm just a college student," or "I'm just a housewife." But ingrained in your gifts and talents is a calling to set people free with the power of Christ. God gave you that authority. The time has come for societies to begin operating by kingdom principles. We need to be aggressive about standing up to the pharaohs and reclaiming places now occupied by the ungodly. Then His dominion will come. Be a Moses! Confront the ungodly when the time is right.

4. Moses raised up other leaders.

Having an impact means more than confronting leaders and trying to influence the powerful. It means raising up other believers to become leaders in every sphere of society. We cannot fold our hands and think that our prayers will convert every leader into a godly person. We can't blindly hope that God will raise up good leaders out of nowhere. No, we are the agents of change. We are to actively raise up God-fearing leaders from our own ranks to have their own impact on society.

Moses was a leader, and he set an example for us by raising up other leaders. Soon after leaving Egypt, Moses "chose able men out of all Israel, and made them heads over the people: rulers of thousands, rulers of hundreds, rulers of fifties, and rulers of tens" (Exod. 18:25, nkjv).

He understood that one person cannot transform a nation

alone. It takes an army of Moseses to restore the kingdom of God to a nation.

In our day, we must help train and direct people in their areas of leadership. As a pastor, I want to help everyone around me find their calling and be successful in life. I make every effort possible, using whatever knowledge I have, to help each person in my life to become a success. I am obliged to help everyone because this is the true nature of God. And this is one of the works God expects us to accomplish. I'm convinced that a pastor's most important task is to help his members become all God made them for.

Kingdom leadership differs from worldly leadership. Worldly leadership is focused on the success of the leader. Kingdom leadership is others focused. Moses was not seeking his own good when he led Israel out of Egypt. Rather, he was seeking the good of the millions who followed him. Let's look at some key distinctions between kingdom leadership and worldly leadership:

- Kingdom leaders try to elevate people by encouraging them and building them up into the people God wants them to be.

- But an ungodly leader rules by control. He restricts those who work beneath him. He controls through excessive rules and regulations, prohibitions, threats, and fear. He doesn't influence people from the inside, and he doesn't encourage or inspire. Rather, he clamps down with external rules designed to keep everybody in line.

- Kingdom leaders use their authority to make others successful. A kingdom leader becomes lower than those he leads so they can "stand" on his shoulders and reach even higher. His followers know that they can put the full weight of their trust on him. He makes himself a ladder that other people climb on their way to success.

- But a worldly leader sees people as tools for his own success. He is always demonstrating this to his people, making them feel that they are nothing in comparison to him, that their positions are less honorable and less prestigious than his. He tries by various means to destroy the potential and capabilities of the people he's been entrusted with. He doesn't give them a chance to develop their talents.

- A kingdom leader is always trying to work himself out of a job. He knows how to trust people and how to delegate authority to fulfill all kinds of tasks. He tries to make himself unnoticed and unnecessary. His goal is to be so effective at raising up other leaders that he himself becomes unneeded.

- But a worldly leader tries to always be indispensable. He sticks his nose into every task that promises to add to his credibility. He makes himself a bottleneck for approval.

Your job as a kingdom leader in any sphere of life is to do as Christ did.

> The Son of Man did not come to be served, but to serve, and to give His life a ransom for many.
> —Matthew 20:28, NKJV

We must raise up godly leaders, just as Jesus did with the apostles and in the early church. We can't afford to be lone rangers if we want to see our nations change for God. Moses learned to raise up leaders, and we must do the same.

5. Moses was insulted by ungodliness.

Some Christians who become leaders in society don't reach their full potential because they are comfortable with the ungodliness around them. They remain complacent because the ungodliness does not sufficiently bother them.

That is not the example of Moses. He was insulted by the ungodliness and unfair treatment he saw in Egypt. That feeling of insult spurred him to do great things for God.

In today's world, ungodliness and evil point their dirty fingers at the church of the living God, daring to challenge her. Pharaohs spurn the church in every country, mocking the people of God. Satan is shouting as loudly as he can through the media and secular culture. He wants to paralyze the church through intimidation. It's as if he is saying, "Try to stop me!" He is strutting around, showing off his supposed stature and size, making us believe all society is with him. We hear the ungodly boasting about their plans to change the laws and standards in their favor.

Many Christians shut the doors of the church and cry and weep and pray, hoping Jesus comes back soon.

But we must become insulted by ungodliness as Moses did. There is a time when holy anger comes up in our souls, when we feel insulted like David felt insulted when Goliath hurled insults at the armies of the living God. We must become insulted by ungodliness in our society. We must have a holy anger at the kingdom of darkness.

Some Christians don't even blink at ungodliness. They hear about ungodliness, but to them it's just news. They don't see it as defiling the earth God is trying to win back to Himself. Where is our outrage? Where is our anger? Where is our sensitivity? The Bible says that when Moses visited Pharaoh to announce the plague on the firstborns, Moses was "hot with anger" (Exod. 11:8). Why aren't we hot with anger about the ungodliness around us?

Are you insulted by ungodliness? Does the ungodly news of the world stoke the fires of righteous anger in you? Or have you become like Lot, accustomed to the ungodliness of Sodom and Gomorrah?

God is raising up leaders who are insulted by ungodliness. They are raising their voice against the devil's taunts. Many of them are coming from unexpected places. They are the outcasts, the migrants, the neglected people, the forgotten, and the childlike. They will not be absorbed by the ungodly culture they find themselves in. Will you respond to the insult of ungodliness as well?

ARE YOU A MAN?

God's definition of a man is different from ours. The prophet said:

> Justice is turned back,
> And righteousness stands afar off;
> For truth is fallen in the street,
> And equity cannot enter.
> So truth fails,
> And he who departs from evil makes himself a prey.
> Then the LORD saw it, and it displeased Him
> That there was no justice.
> He saw that there was no man,
> And wondered that there was no intercessor;
> Therefore His own arm brought salvation for Him;
> And His own righteousness, it sustained Him.
> —**Isaiah 59:14–16**, NKJV

There are several important points in this passage. First, God uses people to carry out His plan for the earth, not angels or any other kind of supernatural being. On Earth, men are His primary means to establish His kingdom. He does not send an angel to do a man's work. Gabriel and Michael are not coming to our rescue. Only men can stop the disgrace of ungodliness.

The second point is that God's definition of a man differs from ours. It says, "He saw that there was no man." Did this mean there were no males around? Of course not. Then what does it mean? Who is a man by God's definition? If we are not men, what are we?

God looks at many of us and does not see "a man." A man brings kingdom solutions to the earth's problems and restores justice and truth. God wants to stop tears and chaos and terror and injustice in our nations. But will He find people He can do it through? Do we fit His criteria?

When God looks down from His throne, what does He see? Men and women ready for service? Or nonentities? Who are you in God's sight? A person ready to impact the life of his nation? Or does He look at you and not see a man?

God calls us "men" only if we identify ourselves with God's kingdom principles. God wants His people to take full responsibility for our nations. Today God is looking at those who are called by His name. Will we become like Moses, leaders and redeemers of nations?

Have you ever gone to the garage looking for a tool and realized that among all the screwdrivers and crowbars and hammers you own, you use relatively few of them? In fact, most of us rely on a few specific tools that seem to work better than others. I think God has the same feeling when looking for people to use. Some Christians just work more effectively than others. It is possible to be both saved and useless. Perhaps God relies on only a few of us. It's dreadful to consider how many times any one of us has been passed over.

I believe God looks upon the earth today and grieves over the condition of mankind. The word *wondered* in this passage does not only mean that the Lord was surprised. It has a much stronger meaning. God was in awe at what He saw. There was no justice, truth, or judgment in the earth. Even worse, there was no intercessor to challenge the present lawlessness. God was very disappointed.

If you are God's representative, you are called to be a man—a true man. Your duty is to stand for His interests and do His will. For this purpose He saved you, paying a very high price—the life of His only begotten Son, Jesus Christ. He stood in the gap to save your soul. Will you stand in the gap for the salvation of the earth? Can He count on you?

Every local church can be a breeding ground for deliverers and Moseses. The church is not for entertaining believers, but it is a place to raise up world changers and history makers. In our church in Kyiv, every member is trained to identify an area of life that he or she will dedicate himself to save and deliver as Moses did. Every believer is a Moses in his or her own sphere. The pastor's role is to lead them into that promised land.

It's time for an army of Moseses to arise and take their place in the nations. This battle is fought using the principles of the kingdom of God to vanquish the kingdom of darkness. In the next chapter I'll share some practical secrets.

KINGDOM PRINCIPLES
FROM CHAPTER 9

1. It's not enough to have large numbers or justice on your side. God needs deliverers like Moses to lead people to victory using wisdom and power. To rule your promised land, you cannot rely on the goodwill of leaders.

2. It's not enough to hide God's Word in your heart. You must speak for God in your place of influence.

3. Sometimes speaking for God means confronting powerful rulers, as Moses did. By confronting unrighteous leaders, you are doing them and your nation a favor.

4. When people do God's will, the heart of the king belongs not only to God but also to the people of the country.

5. We are to actively raise up God-fearing leaders from our own ranks to have their own impact on society.

6. In today's world, ungodliness and evil point their dirty fingers at the church of the living God, daring to challenge her.

7. Every local church can be a breeding ground for deliverers and Moseses. The church is not for entertaining believers, but it is a place to raise up world changers and history makers.

Chapter 10

IMPOSING THE KINGDOM ON THE CULTURE

IN UKRAINE WE HAVE RELIED ON THREE PRACTICAL principles that have given our efforts great effectiveness. These basic principles can transform you and every believer into a kingdom powerhouse.

TEACH HIS PRINCIPLES

In five years, two million people have come to Christ at the altar of our church. We thank God that we are being used to win the lost, but the truly amazing thing is that this has not taken place through evangelism, crusades, or traditional methods of sharing the gospel. Rather, people have come to the church and come to Christ because of the example of many thousands of Christians putting kingdom principles to work outside of the church.

The heart of our discovery is that you don't need to promote religion or church for people to want to come to Christ. Rather, kingdom principles will draw people. You don't even have to mention anything spiritual or religious—in fact, it's sometimes better not to. When you take God's principles into society, they simply work. They draw attention, and people begin to inspect who you are, what motivates you, and what is the philosophy behind your work. Then they discover the kingdom within you, and they become convinced of its truth because they've seen it in action.

Here's how it worked with us. The very first program we launched in our church was aimed at helping drug addicts, alcoholics, and the homeless. To get our message into secular venues like public schools, hospitals, and government institutions we decided to present it in a way to emphasize the principles, not the God behind the principles. We knew the government would never let us into schools if we were waving our Bibles and calling on the name of Jesus. So a woman who was rescued from years of drug addiction and prostitution analyzed the problems of addiction and prostitution and wrote a curriculum based on kingdom principles, without expressly mentioning God.

Public schools allowed her in to share her personal story and to tell students how to avoid falling into such awful traps. She did not preach. She simply taught kingdom principles like integrity, respect, honesty, and so on. The presentation was so successful that schools invited her back many times, and she began to write other programs aimed at helping students withstand peer pressure and abstain from premarital sex. From a church perspective you might say she was teaching holiness in the public schools. But the schools saw it as teaching integrity and respect for fellow human beings. Fine. She was willing to come from their perspective so she could introduce kingdom principles into a setting where a church would never be welcome. This one woman, the former drug addict and prostitute, has since come up with thirty or so programs that have been adopted by public school systems and the ministry of education. Students prefer to attend her presentations instead of going to class. Every week this person who never finished high school reaches more people than all the churches in our city put together.

We saw through her experience that principles unite, but religiosity divides. If I come asking to share about Christ, they won't let me in. But if I say I can help your students be less violent, they welcome me. This is in no way denying God. God is only committed to His Word, which holds His principles. He is not committed to religion or to our particular expression of it. (See Psalm 138:2.) For that reason it's far better to emphasize the integrity of God's kingdom principles and patterns rather than the spirituality of your particular Christian experience. As great as experiences and rituals and manifestations of the Holy Spirit are in our walk with Christ, God has exalted His principles above them. You don't need to bring prayer to schools. You don't need to lay hands on people and pray for them. You don't need to hand out leaflets inviting people to youth group meetings or evangelistic crusades. You can bring kingdom principles to the public sphere in a secular package and receive a far wider hearing. When students stop being violent and stop having children as teenagers, the schools will clamor to have you back.

CREATE MODELS

One of the main activities in our church is the creation of these kinds of programs for societal problems. I often ask for a show of hands during our church services from people who are concerned or knowledgeable about different problems facing our country. People raise their hands, and I ask them to form a committee on the spot. They meet later, write a program, and put it to work. If it's a program to help the jobless, they go to where the jobless are. If it's to help high school students, they go to the high schools. They take the knowledge they have from experience or training and combine it with knowledge of kingdom principles to come up with dynamic solutions. Then they try out the program or presentation in a limited venue to give it a trial run. The success of that trial run becomes a source of boldness to present it to the whole nation. Their small program blooms into a movement that offers a proven solution to a problem. Along the way they register as an organization or charity and become more established and recognized. They gradually become a social force. Soon they are lobbying for kingdom principles in a bigger way than they probably imagined when they first teamed up. Because they are alleviating common social problems, their program receives praise and renown even among non-Christians.

Our members have now started three thousand nongovernment organizations! People in our church have written programs to address smoking, teenage pregnancy, drinking, and much more. Each program helps people to be restored to normal society. At our feeding centers we have lawyers who help people straighten out their documents of citizenship if they are not in order. This establishes them in normal society often for the first time. If they need physical rehabilitation or medical help, we guide them to the right places. People know that every hopeless situation is addressed in our church. For example, our people have started a program to help street children. This has rehabilitated five hundred children in its first decade, returning some to their families. Our Healthy Life-styles program, which is taught to students in Kyiv high schools, teaches young people to discover their purpose and to live responsibly. The program involves parents and teachers as well, promoting a complete solution.

Having organizations that serve society is one of the main reasons our church has grown so quickly. God has given us an exalted position in our country. Though the government for years tried to poison people's minds against us, we have won the battle because most people in the country now have friends or relatives who have been helped by people from our church. Their personal experience trumps the rumors and lies and strengthens our position in society.

The reformation we are experiencing in Ukraine couldn't have been possible without the creation of social organizations founded by Christians. Such organizations give God room to move in the society without giving the government opportunity to clamp down on the church. The government cannot speak against what we are doing because the programs are secular in their approach, though they are in fact based solidly on kingdom principles. As you begin to think of what you might do to change society, remember that God is the solution, but it's OK to present the solution in the way you are allowed, which means emphasizing principles, not spirituality. You are God's representative. Just by being in a place, God is there. You have the anointing and the kingdom answers. Bring it to people in a way you are allowed to. Don't deny them kingdom answers just because you can't speak the name of Jesus. Eventually, kingdom principles will dethrone the kingdom of darkness, like the mustard plant that crowds out other plants. But every big goal starts out small. You start by doing what you can. Give it time to spread simply and naturally through you.

By creating models for solving social problems, you inspire others to do the same. Today in our church, people "own" social problems. We identify with our nation as Moses did his. We take personal responsibility for its ills. For example, Ukraine has a drug problem. Our people no longer see it as a government problem but as our problem. These are our brothers and sisters who are suffering. It is our nation that is paying the price. We are the salt of the earth. If we don't solve the problem, it won't get solved. This is true of the homeless problem, corruption, violence, pornography, and much more. Instead of bemoaning the state of our nation we take responsibility, create programs, register organizations, and start a movement. We are bold enough to believe we are the answer to every problem. That is our evangelism. As a side effect of our efforts, people follow us to church to find the source of our answers. There they find the total solution to their total problem when they meet Jesus and begin living for Him.

Our people have also moved into the political realm because they know that legislation sets the tone and standard for a nation. People from our church lobby the parliament more than any single church. They promote laws against things like public advertisements of pornography, smoking, and drinking. Ukraine is in a particularly important historical moment. When communism fell, it turned every vice loose in our country. Everybody wanted to try everything that had been banned before. It was difficult to preach to people. After years of living under the thumb of Moscow they didn't want any more restrictions. But that is changing, and people are recognizing the need for boundaries in behavior. Today members of our church have indirectly written one hundred forty bills for parliament, including a recent law limiting pornography.

The church needs to use the power it has. God is dissatisfied with our church-minded approach. He created everything, and He wants His principles to rule everywhere. That is your assignment. If you feel called to, say, help homeless people but don't have the guts to start a program yourself, go serve in another man's organization. But in any case, do it! Own the problem, and own the solution.

Creating social organizations and becoming a force in society has another helpful side effect: it protects you from government harassment. Ukraine's governments tried to shut down our church in the past, but when we began owning social problems and providing solutions, it made it much more difficult for them to come against us. Suddenly our people were popping up everywhere: in parliament, in public schools, at homeless shelters, in business. When believers occupy every sphere of life, the government can't do much. So by promoting kingdom principles we also keep our foot in the door of power, lest the door close. And doors do close unexpectedly. If you don't keep flexing your muscle, you may get pushed back.

I am convinced that Christians worldwide occupy less than 1 percent of the positions in society that God has called us to. I was in the United States recently, and during a break in my schedule I was watching *Dr. Phil*, *Montel Williams*, and *Oprah*. I wondered, "Are those talk-show hosts occupying what should be Christian assignments?" These shows raise important topics and stir people up. But Christians have answers. We are kingdom people! We know how this earth is supposed to work. We can bring people to the light. We bring problems to the surface in order to bring truth to bear on it. Some people are building their own empires and bank accounts on the backs of people's problems, but they offer nothing in return. Because Christians have abandoned valid areas of societal concerns, others rush in.

We need to see every position of influence in society as a Christian assignment. We must be more creative, more innovative, more excellent than anyone else. That leads me to the next practical principle of success.

ORGANIZE

Every little idea or inspiration can grow into something big if you know how to care for it. It depends heavily on your organizational skill and your ability to pay attention to small things. Let me point out how Jesus operated:

> Then Jesus said, "Make the people sit down." Now there was much grass in the place. So the men sat down, in number about five thousand. And Jesus took the loaves, and when He had given thanks He distributed them to the disciples, and the disciples to those sitting down; and likewise of the fish, as much as they wanted. So when they were filled, He said to His disciples, "Gather up the fragments that remain, so that nothing is lost." Therefore they gathered them up, and filled twelve baskets with the fragments of the five barley loaves which were left over by those who had eaten. Then those men, when they had seen the sign that Jesus did, said, "This is truly the Prophet who is to come into the world."
>
> —John 6:10–14, nkjv

Jesus performed a great miracle and fed five thousand people with two small fish and five loaves of bread. As soon as He'd finished feeding the people, He drew the disciples' attention to the fragments of bread and fish that were left over. "Gather up the fragments that remain, so that nothing is lost," He told them. But why? Why be concerned about the remaining nubs of food when He could have worked another miracle to create an even larger feast?

I believe Jesus was revealing an aspect of the nature of God to us. God is organized, and He pays attention to small things. Many people lock their attention onto the big vision and forget that a big vision only comes to pass through faithfulness with small things. They neglect organization for the thrill of brainstorming and vision casting.

God is able to make your ideas successful at this very minute, but you would not sustain that success without an effective system of administration, structure, management, and organization. Jesus knew this. That's why He sent the disciples out to gather everything that had been left over after the meal. Jesus was indicating that nothing is to be wasted. Even the way He managed the miracle in the first place shows us God's nature. When He wanted to feed the people, He told them to sit down in an orderly way. Without structure, management, and organization, no miracle will bear lasting fruit.

God tells us something seemingly contradictory in Proverbs 13:23: "Much food is in the tillage of the poor: but there is that is destroyed for want of judgment" (KJV). This seems like a contradiction. How can there be rich harvest and the person is still poor? The fact is, God gives a lot even to the poor. But people remain poor when they manage it poorly. Some people have amazing ideas and wonderful plans, but their lack of organization dooms their effectiveness. They never get past the idea stage.

In the first year of our existence as a church, we had a financial problem. Our annual income was two thousand dollars, but we needed five thousand dollars just to pay for the building we were renting. I cried out to God, asking Him to meet our need, and God answered, "The problem is not that you haven't got any fat offerings. Rather, start being careful with every cent you have. Check your petty expenditure account and keep it under control." I became much stricter and more meticulous about how we spent our church money. That lesson prepared us for greater effectiveness.

Some false religious organizations find success not through the truth of their message but because of their organizational skills. I can think of several cults that manage their resources so effectively that they are growing faster than most denominations. There is a so-called church in Kyiv that attracts mostly young people. This church denies some key biblical tenets, but it continues to grow because it has a well-thought-out organization.

I was ignorant of the importance of organization when I first became a pastor. I thought that to be successful I just had to have an anointing and a powerful word, and to know how to pray and preach well. I reckoned that if I had all that, I could be a successful minister. But now I know better. At least half of any organization's success comes from—being well organized! You won't be effective in any endeavor unless you also have a well-thought-out structure.

At one point in the early life of our church, at least thirty thousand people had made a decision for the Lord. But afterward many of them went back into the world again. We blamed this on the difficulties we had with finding a building that was large enough to accommodate our Sunday services. But I came to see that that wasn't the real reason. Our lack of organizational structure was to blame. It shattered me that thirty thousand people had made decisions for the Lord in our church and yet we had not been able to keep them. The deficiency was in me. When I discovered that I was unable to organize and lead the church properly, I called our pastors together and shared this problem with them. I started working to become a better manager by reading books about organization and management. I invited a businessman to our church council meeting to offer suggestions about organizing a system and creating structures.

Since that time we have become much more organized, and I believe that has been a key in our effectiveness. God cannot build on a sloppy structure. Your great ideas for advancing God's kingdom will founder on the shores of disorganization unless you become a master manager of resources and people.

If you have more inspiration than organization, do as I did: seek out the knowledge and people who will help to make your idea successful. The programs that have been most effective in the world have been led by organized people. Follow Jesus's example: manage your miracles well. Let nothing be lost. Pay special attention to small things because they are the building blocks of bigger things.

As I mentioned earlier, my study of sociology, anthropology, and psychology have taught me that every modern society can be divided into seven spheres of influence:

1. Spiritual/social
2. Government/politics

3. Business/economy
4. Education
5. Media
6. Culture/entertainment
7. Sports

If we infiltrate all these spheres of influence and their hundreds of subdivisions, we will have brought the kingdom lifestyle to a whole nation.

So in Ukraine, all our teaching and training in church are directed at helping every believer to identify and adopt a particular area of influence according to his or her passion until that sphere of life is totally permeated with the principles of the kingdom of God. The only reason they come to church is to be further imbued with the nature of God, so as to bring it to bear on their sphere of influence. They come to be trained in principles and values of the kingdom they will use to change their world from Monday to Friday.

It is never too late to do your part in impacting your sphere of influence through the application of kingdom principles. The kingdom of God comes not primarily through preaching, which is just a means of training and preparation. The kingdom comes to others through your passion and gifting. Teach His principles, create models, and be organized. I can almost assure you that as you do, your effectiveness will increase a hundredfold and more.

KINGDOM PRINCIPLES
FROM CHAPTER 10

1. Principles unite, but religiosity divides. It is far better to emphasize the integrity of God's kingdom principles and patterns rather than the spirituality of your particular Christian experience.

2. You can bring kingdom principles to the public sphere in a secular package and receive a far wider hearing.

3. Eventually, kingdom principles will dethrone the kingdom of darkness, like the mustard plant that crowds out other plants.

4. By creating models for solving problems, you inspire others to do the same. Instead of bemoaning the state of our nation, we take responsibility, create programs, register organizations, and start a movement.

5. When believers occupy every sphere of life, the government can't do much. By promoting kingdom principles, we also keep our foot in the door of power, lest the door close.

6. God is organized, and He pays attention to small things. Without structure, management, and organization, no miracle will bear lasting fruit. The programs that have been most effective in the world have been led by organized people.

7. The kingdom comes to others through your passion and gifting.

Chapter 11

WHEN TO
STOP PRAYING

I AM A FIRM BELIEVER IN PRAYING—AND IN NOT praying. The first part of this chapter is about knowing when to pray. The second is about knowing when not to pray. You must learn both skills to be effective in your promised land.

If there is anything I could choose to be a hallmark of my life, it is prayer. It was said about Jesus that He prayed a lot. I too have endeavored to live my life through prayer. I have disciplined myself at times to spend weeks in prayer, interrupted only by sleep. Those times have changed my life. They are spent absorbing His presence, His glory, and His strength. I have never prayed for the sake of praying. I have prayed because I want to be with God, to get to know Him, and then to radiate His glory. To me, this is the point of my life. Everything else seems to me like a hobby.

Action without prayer is foolish. Even if your intentions are good, even if you are trying to build God's kingdom, you cannot succeed without prayer. Prayer is not merely a habit but a way of life. We can commune constantly with God. Learn to lay your soul bare before God. Learn to humble yourself before Him in prayer. Learn to admit your weaknesses, your mistakes in His presence. Put your trust in Him. He is your hope, your source, your life. All else could fail, but having Him, you have everything. Let Him know that you are trusting completely in Him. Fast so as to humble your flesh.

Learn also to wait on the Lord. It's important not just to storm the heavens with your prayers, but to rest in God and to be guided by His assessment of the situation, relying on Him in everything. God always gives grace to the person who humbles himself before Him and who sets his hopes on Him. No matter what defeats that person may suffer, God makes it possible for him to spread his wings and mount up to new heights. God will equip him supernaturally and show him how to remain standing even when others fall. As the prophet wrote:

> Even youths grow tired and weary,
>   and young men stumble and fall;
> but those who hope in the Lord
>   will renew their strength.
> They will soar on wings like eagles;
>   they will run and not grow weary,
>   they will walk and not be faint.

—Isaiah 40:30–31

RECEIVE REVELATION

In prayer you learn who God is and what He wants you to do. Jesus said, "By myself I can do nothing" (John 5:30). With these words He reaffirmed His humility and total dependence on His Father. And God the Father, seeing this gesture of humility, gave further grace to the Son.

The revelations you receive are like foundation stones upon which you can build your life, family, and calling according to God's plan. The revelations you receive in prayer will unveil the prototype or picture of what you should do next. If you put these revelations into action according to His model, you will walk a well-trodden pathway and not just go around in circles.

In some ways I have grown to be an observer in my church. In times of prayer and throughout the day I simply observe what the Father does, and I observe those around me to be sure they are carrying it out according to the revelation God gives us. Some pastors claim that it's difficult to be a pastor of a large congregation. But it isn't that difficult for me; it's a light burden, almost like being on vacation. Prayer makes it so.

If you receive a word of revelation and have an understanding of what God is wanting to build and the unique way in which He is going to bring what He has in mind to pass; if you take the steps He is expecting you to take, then your life and calling become light. You will find pleasure and great delight in them. It's no longer you who is building, but God. He goes before you, accomplishing the things He has called and appointed you for. You have only to be an obedient doer of His will. The things you build in the here and now will have already been built in heaven, and you will simply be establishing them.

I can say without exception that every major decision or advance in my life has come following sustained times of prayer. For example, I prayed a lot before I got married. Six whole years passed, and still nothing changed in my life. One day, however, I prayed and heard, as it were, in a dream, "Write down what you need." I quickly wrote down the things I desired and was turning over in my mind concerning the kind of wife I wanted. I wrote down ten points and realized that this was the Spirit of God moving me to write these things. They were things He wanted to give me. He allowed me to perceive the prototype He had prepared for me. As I wrote down these ten points, I realized that these would help me know my future wife from thousands of other women. I would know which one she was, because God had given me a "portrait" of her personality. Within a year, I found the unique person that God had destined to be my wife. She met all ten points God had given me.

THEN STOP PRAYING

Sometimes people pray without ever taking action. There is a time to leave the prayer room and carry out the plans God has revealed to you. For too many years some Christians have concentrated on prayer only. They believe that God will supernaturally accomplish what they are asking for. But the Word of God says that faith without works is useless and dead, according to James 2:17. The kingdom does not advance on prayer alone, but on prayer-inspired actions.

You will recall that when our church was needing a permanent place to meet, we prayed for a year and God was silent. That silence bothered me terribly. I couldn't understand why we had prayed and God hadn't done anything. I was still expecting God to do everything for us. I wasn't putting my faith into action. Finally, God had mercy on me and told me that prayer doesn't do anything by itself. "No matter how much you pray, it's not in My hands," God spoke to my heart. "The solution is in your hands. I have given you the opportunity. The people of the world don't understand prayer. They understand the language of force. Prayer is for Me, and this is not My situation. It is within your scope of influence to change it. You are on the earth; you have the people and the power. Use your power."

It was time for us to quit praying, and we did. Our actions led to a favorable resolution to our problem and eventually led to a change in the entire nation. But many people still cling to old ways. They are almost idolatrous of prayer. The other day I was listening to an interview with Christian leaders in Nigeria. They were asked why the country was not well developed even though it has many Christians. The leaders said, "We need to pray more." Can you imagine! Nigeria is one of the most prayerful countries on the planet. They pray constantly. But countries don't develop by prayer but by prayer paired with actions.

It reminds me of the time God told Moses, "Get up! What are you doing on your face? Take action." (See Exodus 14:15.) Praying and interceding are critical, but they are only half of the equation. Why is God silent in your life? Perhaps because He is waiting for you to act! In that chilling silence perhaps you will learn to take action with the power you already have.

TIMID WARRIORS

Many church-minded Christians are timid and passive but think they're being humble. They devote themselves to prayer, but they are really just avoiding the battle. People hide in the prayer closet, as Saul hid in the luggage on his coronation day, or Gideon hid in the winepress. Many are afraid of the consequences of taking risks. They don't want to feel pain. This fear, like all fear, is rooted in egocentrism. When you are not dead to yourself, you fear the consequences of failure. Egocentrism masquerades as humility and practical thinking. But it's focused on yourself and what causes you pain. That's called serving your own comfort. You are not looking out for kingdom interests but your own.

True humility goes where God leads, regardless of the consequences. It recognizes that we are dead to ourselves, but alive in Christ. We don't live our own lives anymore. We were headed for hell when He rescued us. So we don't call the shots anymore; He does. His will is our command, no matter if it brings us life or death.

I'm convinced that 75 percent of our prayers are a waste of time. Either we are praying for something God has already said yes to, or we are praying for something He told us to do. We are waiting on God while He is waiting on us! I often hear people say they are expecting a miracle and waiting on God for an answer. Waiting on God is good, to a point. Then it's time to stop expecting miracles and start taking action on the revelation we have received thus far.

If you are a timid warrior, you will not take the land God has for you. Your position in society will shrink, and the kingdom of God will lose territory because of you. You may be a giant in the prayer closet but a pipsqueak on the battlefield. Stop escaping into prayer! Be a prayer warrior but not a prayer hermit.

The kingdom belongs to doers, not hearers. You can hear God speak all you want, but if you don't do anything, the kingdom does not rightly belong to you. The developing world is a great example of this. In many third world countries Christians have succeeded in getting people saved and into church. There, people dance and worship and pray before God, but those same countries lack kingdom principles in the government, businesses, and social structure of the nation. Some countries are full of faithful believers living in poverty. Nothing changes for the better. The world of the Christians never collides with the world around them. On the other hand, some nonbelieving countries are wealthy, well organized, and just, but no longer acknowledge the Lord.

It's time to bloody our swords (metaphorically speaking). The prophet said:

Cursed is he who does the work of the LORD deceitfully,
And cursed is he who keeps back his sword from blood.
—Jeremiah 48:10, NKJV

Every calling requires dedication. Unless you dedicate yourself to your calling, you will not go far. I know many gifted people who have been called by God. But without dedication, they soon fizzle out. God absolutely loathes it when a person has a noncommittal attitude toward His work. If a person is frivolous toward God's work, he puts himself under a curse, as it says above. The word *deceitfully* there means literally "slack, negligently." This is serious business. Whatever you do, do it heartily as to the Lord. Cursed is everyone who does the work of the Lord negligently. If you have not been conscientious in your work for God, repent and take a different attitude toward your calling. If you expect everything to work itself out and think you can just sit back and rest, I can guarantee you will soon have plenty of difficulties. Do not expect a harvest if you haven't sown anything.

There are times when you must pull out your sword to carry out your calling. Not everything is attained easily. The kingdom of God advances by violence. Christians are made strong by the Word of God, but many attain absolutely nothing because they are not willing to fight. God didn't tell Joshua to defeat his enemies with prayer alone. He said, "Be strong and courageous," and then He sent him onto the battlefield (Josh. 10:25). When we keep back the sword from blood, it turns on us and destroys us. We have to know how to fight and advance the kingdom. When the devil tells you, "No!" you have to be able to tell him, "Yes!" When everyone around you says, "Impossible!" you have to be in a position to say, "It is possible! By faith it will surely come to pass."

One of the most powerful words in the Great Commission is the word *go* (Matt. 28:18–20). *Go* is also the most neglected word in the church today. Churches try to bring in as many members as possible to sit and listen to our beautiful rhetoric week in and week out. This is the direct opposite of Christ's instruction to us, which is to get people saved, train them, and release them to change the world they came from. That is why in our church I always tell my members that my job and my dream is to "chase" them out of their pews to the harvest field of the world where they all belong. One of my most important duties as a pastor is to just get people to "go"!

You have been given your promised land so that you can fight and take it victoriously. If you have a calling from the Lord and do nothing to fulfill it, you are on the verge of being ruined. It is not your work but God's. He has entrusted you with it. You are called to battle. There is no need to keep back your sword from blood. There is a time for you to pray and a time for you to fight. If you have been working with too little for too long, then you probably haven't been faithful. You need to exit the prayer closet and step onto the battlefield. By definition, if you are faithful with little, you will graduate to much. Nobody is supposed to muddle around with little things his whole life. You were made for bigness. Until you have done everything you can think or imagine, God won't swing into action on your behalf. He gave you a mind so you can think great thoughts and an imagination so you can imagine what could be. Until you use these God-given tools, don't expect Him to intervene. You must be faithful with what's within your capabilities before you can expect a miracle.

When you have pulled out your sword, gone into battle, and put actions to the revelations you received in prayer, then you can expect God to do more than you could think or imagine. Learn to be a man or woman of prayer. Then learn when to stop praying. The results will be powerful.

KINGDOM PRINCIPLES
FROM CHAPTER 11

1. I have prayed because I want to be with God, to get to know Him, and then to radiate His glory.

2. Action without prayer is foolish.

3. The revelations you received are like foundation stones upon which you can build your life, family, and calling according to God's plan.

4. The kingdom does not advance on prayer alone but on prayer-inspired actions. Countries don't develop but by prayer paired with actions.

5. When you are not dead to yourself, you fear the consequences of failure.

6. True humility goes where God leads, regardless of the consequences. His will is our command, no matter if it brings us life or death.

7. The kingdom belongs to doers, not hearers. One of my most important duties as a pastor is to just get people to "go"! There is a time for you to pray and a time for you to fight.

Chapter 12

THE ORANGE
REVOLUTION

OUR BOLD MARCH ON CITY HALL IN THE SPRING of 2004 gave our church a major victory in the face of potential danger. Before that time our church was not permitted to own land. Now the government gave us a large piece of property right in the city. It didn't cost us a dime. Standing up to the authorities became another step on our journey that would transform our nation. But in a breathtakingly short time, God went much further and used our example to start a political revolution that changed Ukraine's government.

RUMBLINGS OF DISCONTENT

In November 2004, six months after our march, Ukraine held presidential elections. Unlike in the United States and other Western countries, where elections are mostly transparent, fair, and democratic, Ukraine's elections were still a murky business. The candidate of the established, Moscow-backed government represented the old, heavy-handed, and corrupt way of doing things. His opponent was Victor Yushchenko, who represented democracy and a more open, servant-hearted leadership.

The election was very close, and a runoff was held between the established candidate and the challenger Yushchenko. When the votes were counted, it became clear that Yushchenko had won. But the current government leaders were rigging the vote count to keep themselves in office. This did not surprise anyone. It was common for sitting governments to steal elections in our part of the world. But this time the political and socioeconomic atmosphere of Ukraine was as explosive as a tinderbox. People had tired of corruption and chaos in their leaders. Bureaucracy and a deficient executive had led many people to absolute poverty. Social problems had worsened to the point of crisis: street children, drug addiction, alcoholism, crime, prostitution, and AIDS were ravaging the country but not being addressed. The Ukrainian people, many living on the edge of poverty, spent their lives working for the benefit of a small group of people who were in power. The corrupt system gave ordinary citizens no legal recourse. Minimum wages were barely enough to keep people from starving. Ludicrously low pensions humiliated the elderly people who had worked all their lives for the country. Young people saw no future for themselves.

This contrasted with the millions of dollars of the so-called new Ukrainians who considered themselves the elite of society, but who were taking the wealth of the country for themselves through corruption and unjust laws.

So when the government tried to rig the election, people quickly realized they were being ripped off. But this time they took action. For decades our country had been frozen solid, paralyzed, and afraid. The communist mind-set still ruled. But our church's march on city hall, which was widely reported and criticized in the major media, had had a strong positive effect as well. It had warmed up the spiritual climate in the whole country. People saw that if you wanted things to change, you must stand up for your rights. You must demonstrate the justness of your cause. The country has seen us call for righteousness and openness in our leaders, and instead of being greeted by bullets and tanks, the leaders gave us what we asked for. Our actions helped to clear the fear from people's minds. Boldness came to everyday Ukrainians. They began to dream of freedom. They developed a willingness to fight for their rights. They saw that the government is to serve the people, not hold them captive like cattle.

As the newspapers and television reported that the established candidate had "won," the nation shook off its paralysis. People spontaneously took to the streets and gathered in Independence Square, the main city square in Kyiv. Hundreds of thousands of citizens left their jobs and homes to stand up for what was right. There were many Moseses in Ukraine. They rose up to guide the future of their nation. People from our church went out by the thousands to stand with the country to defend the integrity of the elections. Soon half a million people crowded into Independence Square. We adopted orange as our symbol of protest. It was a symbol of spring, new beginnings, and new brightness in the heart of Ukraine. Even though we were met by soldiers with guns, we were convinced of the justness of our cause.

FORETOLD BY GOD

As a church we had been expecting some sort of major social change for more than a year. I had prophesied several times that God was about to do something great in Ukraine. In March 2003 I said publicly, "God is opening the heaven over Ukraine. The nation, which was humiliated, will start rising again. Thus says the Lord, 'Hitherto were you abased, but now by My sovereignty will I start lifting you up. I tell every humiliated one now, start moving boldly, start moving firmly, start moving bravely because your God will go in advance of you.'"

Leading up to the election our church fasted and prayed for months for a good outcome. This tradition of relying on fasting and prayer went back to 1997 when we began holding two yearly fasts, plus monthly three-day fasts, during which we interceded for our country. The summer fast of that very year, 2004, was dedicated to the presidential elections to come. We had prepared well in prayer. During the revolution itself, four thousand of our members prayed and fasted for the potentially violent standoff to be resolved.

In March 2004, God had confirmed that He was about to do something in our country by sending another prophecy. On that day I said these words:

Soon the whole Ukraine will be celebrating, because the Spirit of God will take over all the spheres of society and will triumph over every iniquity, lawlessness, and sin. God will subdue every name under the heavens and will manifest His omnipresent glory in this country. He will shake the top and the bottom. He will shake the economy and the polity. He will shake the country until every knee bows before Him!

God will visit Ukraine, and it will be an appearance of His glory and grace. It will be a sovereign act of God! It will not depend on a person or a particular church. God Himself will visit this country. He will raise up Ukraine.

God will visit Ukraine, and nobody can stand in the way to prevent it from happening. No man can prevent it. The devil can't prevent it. God has decided to move, and He will move. God will start raising ministers in all spheres of society. Politicians will start preaching. Businessmen and bankers will serve God. The celebrities will worship Him. I prophesy this with the power of the Holy Spirit in the name of Jesus Christ.

Ukraine will change! It doesn't matter how much time will pass; it will take place. Our children and grandchildren will walk the streets safely because God's protection will be this country's covering.

Ukraine will be shaken up by the power of God. This country will find out that God is real, and He is in the people business. Everybody will know that God is the master of this earth, and you can't mess around with Him. He doesn't want to tolerate sin and lawlessness in this land. God will reveal Himself so that His truth reigns. People will start to change and reconsider their standings. Many will see that only with God, who is alive today, the future is possible. Ukraine will be filled with the evangelical movement, the movement of transformation, bringing many to repentance. People will turn to God even without preaching the gospel and will be hungry to know Him. Everyone living in Ukraine will get to know about God's supremacy.

God has already made the decision to visit this country. God Himself will touch people's hearts, and they will bow down before Him and turn to Him in prayer. Believers of all denominations and confessions will begin each day with a corporate prayer. God's mighty hand will be seen in this.

God is looking for individuals whom He can trust, who will lead the people. God is looking for someone to reveal His glory through.

We, as Christians, have the privilege before the people of the world to boast of the name of the Lord, to rejoice and be proud and celebrate that we are fortunate to be chosen by Him. You will be the witnesses of these events, and you will remember my words. You will be the history makers because God is opening the heavens over Ukraine!

God will start raising the oppressed and humiliated by His sovereign will. He Himself will go before them. God will do incredible things through these people, things they haven't even dreamt of. People who thought that they weren't chosen will appear among those chosen. God will raise many a Moses in the social, political, spiritual, scientific, and artistic spheres. He will raise people who will be able to resist the present-time pharaohs by the power of the living God. Nobody will be able to oppose God's chosen people, because no power can stop or over-throw God's power in this country. Ukraine will know

that there is one God and master of the earth—Jesus
Christ!

This prophecy prepared my heart and the hearts of many others
for what was to come. When it did come, we welcomed it and
threw ourselves into support of our country.

REVOLUTION!

In that glorious winter of 2004, hundreds of thousands of us gathered in Independence Square to protest the unfair results of the
presidential election. It was the most wonderful revolution any
country had ever seen. Not a drop of blood would be shed. There
were no angry mobs fomenting revenge. There were no would-be
Lenins or mavericks shouting through megaphones. Rather, the
people were singing, dancing, laughing, and handing out flowers
to the police guards.

Huge crowds in the square chanted "Yushchenko!" and "We
are for a fair vote!" They openly disputed the falsification of the
vote count, accused the officials of breaking election laws, and
demanded that the government resign and nullify the results of
the central election committee, which had stolen the victory from
Yushchenko. People stayed in Independence Square day and night,
playing music, giving speeches, chanting uplifting slogans, waving
giant orange flags and flags of Ukraine, and holding up big banners
and colorful balloons. At night the square was alight with candles.
Patriotism and pride in our nation swelled in every heart. People
dyed their hair and their beards orange to show their support of
our Orange Revolution.

What was happening in the streets of Kyiv may have appeared strange to some, but it was familiar to people who attended our church and other Protestant churches. There was freedom, joy, love, dancing, music, and celebration of righteousness. Nobody was violent. It was perhaps the most joyful revolution in modern times. The government was so amazed by what was happening that they accused our church of hypnotizing the country and making everyone unreasonably happy. They thought we used black magic because the mood of the protesters was just like what government spies had seen in our church. They thought we had orchestrated this massive protest, but it was the Holy Spirit who had done it. We were just trying to keep up with His work.

People from our church took an active role in sustaining the revolution in many ways. They donated food, warm clothing, and tents to the thousands of demonstrators camped in Kyiv's freezing Independence Square. Our church erected a tent chapel in Independence Square and offered shelter to thousands of people who were protesting. Some people slept there; others received medication, warm clothing, and food. Pastors, leaders, and church members were on 'round-the-clock duty in the tent. Thirty of our church members cooked hot meals to feed the protesters in the square. Some of our members served in Yushchenko's campaign.

But above all, people needed spiritual food during that turbulent time. The Embassy of God had published a newspaper outlining God's principles for the national transformation of Ukraine according to kingdom principles. During the revolution more than half a million copies were handed out to Ukrainians, fueling their hunger for spiritual awakening that went beyond political revolution.

A special spirit reigned in the capital of Ukraine during those days. The Spirit of God filled people's hearts with mercy and compassion for their neighbors. Kyivites shared everything they had with those who came to the capital. People took shifts to be in the square. They hosted total strangers in their homes and took care of the inhabitants of the tent city that had spontaneously sprung up in Khreshatik, a street that crosses Independence Square.

I stayed often with the people of Ukraine in Independence Square. During those days more than ten thousand members of our church held two meetings on the central streets of the city. They prayed for Ukraine and its future, for the peaceful settlement of the conflict, and for the healing and unity of the eastern and western regions of the country. Then, for the very first time in history of Ukraine, representatives from different Christian denominations—Orthodox, Catholic, and Protestant—gathered in the square to pray every morning for the settlement of the situation in Ukraine and for the triumph of justice in the land. The events of those days brought a spiritual unity our country had never seen in its history.

In spite of the alarming news emanating from the government headquarters, the people in the square were constantly filled with an inexplicable joy. The nation could not be overcome by evil anymore, for God had come to our land. It was His hand that restrained the army and military forces and kept the protests peaceful. At one point young girls brought flowers to the thousands of soldiers and special police divisions forming the shield walls against the protest. These men were prepared to fire on command, but these girls approached them without any fear. They glowed with God's love and human dignity as they gave them the flowers. It was breathtaking. God Himself was moving on the hearts of the Ukrainian people. It was not just an Orange Revolution but a spiritual revolution. We were not just standing against an unfair vote count but against evil and wickedness in all positions of power and all spheres of society. In the square, as we waited for the government to respond to our demands, we chanted, "God is with us, and nothing can overcome us."

After two weeks, the revolution achieved its victory. The events in Independence Square finished peacefully. The results of the rigged vote count were nullified, and the challenger Yushchenko was declared the victor. The world joined with us by television in our joyous celebration. The police and military forces never fired a shot. Now they smiled and received hot tea from the girls who had previously brought them flowers. It reminded me of the verse in Proverbs that says:

> When a man's ways are pleasing to the Lord,
> he makes even his enemies live at peace with him.
>
> **—Proverbs 16:7**

On that day I told the people, "Our church is not separate from the nation. The church is with its nation. We are not standing aside and remaining aloof. Thousands of members are here today and many thousands of believers from other churches. This is the triumph not only of the revolution but of freedom and the rights of man."

NEW BEGINNING

After the revolution, Ukraine entered a new era. The change in the mind-set of the people completely changed the political atmosphere in the country. In January 2005, President Yushchenko amazed the nation by starting his first day in office with public prayer. He and his wife and children bowed their knees before an altar. Gathered with them were representatives of all the Christian denominations, including Protestant churches that were once considered cults in Ukrainian society. Now they stood together blessing the president on his first day in office.

After his victory, Yushchenko thanked us with a plaque of appreciation, saying, "Your conscientious work has become a considerable part in that victory. It was you who protected democracy in Ukraine, standing for its high ideals, not considering your own interests. I am convinced that as long as there are people in Ukraine who have the same civil position, dignity, and spirit as you have, everything will be all right in this country." This plaque hangs in my office to this day.

Suddenly the political dialogue of our country changed. Politicians were speaking in spiritual terms about the health and unity of our country and the role of God in our nation. In an interview in 2005, Yushchenko himself told the nation that "the lack of spiritual unity in Ukraine over the last ten to fourteen years is influencing every aspect of life, especially politically. I'm convinced that if we would have had more spiritual politicians, many of the things you heard about over the last months...would have been stopped by the faith of those politicians."

A member of the parliament told the media in a 2004 press

conference, "I know beyond a shadow of a doubt that nothing good can happen in Ukraine if a strong Christian movement doesn't come and establish its principles in society. Without Christian principles we can't manage to build something good."

Yushchenko's inauguration was a day of celebration for us all. In his speech he told the nation, "Today Ukraine is free and independent. We have shrugged off the heavy load of the past. No longer will someone tell us how we should live and for whom we should vote." We shouted a hearty amen to that.

He then declared the beginning of a new life in the country—a life without corruption, crime, deceit, and indignation. His inauguration turned into a magnificent event that filled Independence Square with the outpouring of God's love, joy, and feeling of triumph of His principles in the land. Yushchenko expressed abundant thanks to God.

During his first months in office, Christians were delighted with Yushchenko's unprecedented stand against corruption. He appointed many sincere Christian believers to be his ministers, including the minister of culture, the head of National Security of Ukraine, and others.

A woman named Julia Timoshenko became the new prime minister of Ukraine. She is a woman of outspoken faith, and because of her influence, God's principles have permeated many government programs. She is dedicated to the spiritual development of the Ukrainian nation, especially the new generation. In a 2005 inaugural speech for the Cabinet of Ministers, she told a gathering of our country's leaders, "It is not God who needs our faith, but individuals and society that need it. I am absolutely certain that Ukraine will never rise up until she kneels before God."

But the old government leaders were not ready to give up that easily. They argued before the Supreme Court in January 2005 to try to have Yushchenko removed and their Moscow-supported candidate declared president. They singled out our church for particular blame. "An undeniable fact is that they used psychological methods and led massive groups of people into states of trance and superficial hypnosis, like the Embassy of God sect does, for example," the government's lawyer told the justices, according to the official record. "By the way, the Embassy of God was [in the Square] supporting the presidential candidate, Victor Yushchenko. Also, we can't ignore the conclusion of the mayor of Kyiv made during the meeting where he considered that unfortunately, all the residents of Ukraine at [Independence Square] were hypnotized."

These lawyers even showed the justices a copy of our church newspaper. But the hearing ended with their defeat. The Supreme Court upheld Yushchenko's victory, and the last gasps of the Soviet-style power grab were snuffed out.

THE FRUITS OF FREEDOM

Ukraine today is a country blessed by God. The Lord trusted us to be participants in great historical events. We lived the Bible verse that says, "Remove the wicked from the king's presence, and his throne will be established through righteousness" (Prov. 25:5).

Our land, which was in darkness for seventy years, took the side of truth and is now experiencing God's blessing. The people of Ukraine see a great future. The newly elected government has an enormous amount of trust among the citizens. We are convinced that the government will help to lead the country to prosperity by applying God's principles.

But even better than a changed government are the changed hearts of the people. The Ukrainian people have tasted the fruits of freedom and will not allow anyone to deprive us of it anymore. Spiritual revival has stirred in all spheres of the country, among everyone from ordinary citizens to the highest government leaders. People see no place for wickedness, corruption, bribery, or theft. Followers of God are taking key positions in the government. The oligarchical clans that once controlled the country's wealth and property through under-the-table deals have been smashed.

But we also have seen firsthand that in times of spiritual and social revival, divine justice still operates. God's punishment comes to everyone who does evil things, and sometimes it comes quickly. The Bible says, "It is a fearful thing to fall into the hands of the living God" (Heb. 10:31, NKJV).

For example, on December 3, 2004, the president of the Credit Bank of Ukraine, a financier for the old government, died under mysterious conditions. On December 27, 2004, the minister of transport and communications of the old regime suddenly died. On March 5, 2005, the former minister of internal affairs died in a mysterious suicide. Nobody can say for certain that God's hand was in these events, but the timing seemed to indicate that the old order had passed.

On the other side, God was lifting up believers into positions of prominence. In parliamentary elections a member of the Embassy of God was elected mayor of Kyiv, and his party won 20 percent of the city parliament seats. This mayor rose to prominence thanks in part to his coordination of our church's food distribution program in

Kyiv's poor neighborhoods. Ukraine is 75 percent Orthodox Christian, and Kyiv is proud to be the motherland of the Russian Orthodox Church; yet the growing influence of the Protestant churches can no more be denied. In this last election, more than one thousand believers ran for various posts all over the country. They are now bringing the values and standards of the kingdom to their political offices. Thanks to these Moseses, God's principles have come to the highest levels of society.

Today, the spiritual climate of Ukraine is being revived. Churches and cathedrals are being restored. God is bringing Ukraine back to its former glory. Our country has much to share with the world, for God has blessed us with abundant natural and spiritual resources. For a long time the wealth belonged to the oligarchs who did ungodly things and cared only for their own interests. Now the wealth is available to all the people, through diligence and hard work.

Ours is a land chosen by God for this moment in history. In the very beginning of Christianity, history tells us that the apostle Andrew ministered in the land where Kyiv is situated today and prophesied that God would show special favor to the people of Ukraine and would raise up many churches in this country. I believe we are living the fulfillment of that prophecy.

There are still many battles to fight. Recently, the BBC visited us and ran a news story about our church that aired around the world. It was a positive report, but a Russian Orthodox priest was quoted on camera saying about us, "The followers become like zombies. They are fully devoted to the leader of the organization. They are ready to fulfill any of his desires." He is exactly right that our people are fully devoted to their leader, but the leader is not me—it's Jesus!

What is happening in Ukraine is God-inspired, but it need not be unique. God has ordained similar revolutions for each nation and each individual. The Lord wants every person to find a promised land and learn to rule it by kingdom principles. The world is waiting desperately for us to do so.

KINGDOM PRINCIPLES
FROM CHAPTER 12

1. When you are obedient to God's guidance, He can literally shake the foundations of your nation.

2. When the church takes a strong, visible stance in society, godly people will more easily rise to positions of influence and power.

3. God may have a bigger change in mind for your sphere of influence than you currently realize.

Chapter 13

THE WORLD IS
WAITING FOR YOU

R ECENTLY I WAS INVITED TO ATTEND THE HIGH
profile Clinton Global Initiative meeting in
New York City. We met to exchange ideas about
solving global problems. At this meeting of the world's most
powerful people, I conversed with Madeleine Albright,
Colin Powell, Richard Branson, the mayor of London,
England, former heads of state, Desmond Tutu, and many
other leaders. Everywhere I turned, there was a recognizable
person. The setting was so informal that you could walk up
to anyone and introduce yourself, which I did.

But as I looked around I saw very few church leaders. In fact,
I can only recall seeing one other pastor there, the pastor of a large
and well-known church in the United States. During the entire

event I wondered why this was so. I found my answer while talking to former president Bill Clinton. I wanted to know why I had been invited, so I asked him how he had heard about me and what I had done to merit being with all these bona fide leaders.

He told me, "I know about you. I like what I read about you. I love what you're doing."

His answer spoke volumes to me about the state of the church. I had been invited because he had read about our church. If our church were only solving internal church disputes and concentrating on personal growth, nobody would have cared about me. But because we have stepped into the kingdom role God has called us to, I was counted among the most powerful people in the world—at least for those few days.

It was a privilege to participate in that summit, but it also broke my heart. I nearly wept at how irrelevant Christians have become. Believers, by and large, are so buried in their churches that they are invisible to the rest of the world. We disengage from the world and still claim to be doing kingdom work. Even worse is how we criticize people who are doing kingdom work. People like Bill Clinton and rock star Bono are putting kingdom principles to work, yet people condemn Bono because he doesn't act like American evangelicals, and they criticize Clinton at any opportunity because they don't like his politics or personal behavior. Bono's efforts have resulted in billions of dollars going toward poverty-abatement programs, and Clinton's global initiative is addressing problems God wants solved: alleviating poverty, improving health, stopping religious and ethnic conflict, and taking proper care of the earth. We may disagree with their means to solving these problems, but most church leaders have not even addressed these issues.

They're on the sidelines. In fact, they're not even in the stadium. These problems mean life or death for countless millions. They mean much more than what color the carpet in the chapel is, or who will sing in the worship band. But the Christian community is largely mute on the major issues of the day.

As a result, God has passed over many believers. The people meeting to discuss issues of national and international importance are, for the most part, not Christians. Yet they carry God's burden for the poor, the unhealthy, the prisoner, the orphan, and the downtrodden. They are doing exactly what Jesus would do. But we are like the Levite and the priest in the story of the good Samaritan. Both passed by the dying man. Both apparently were too caught up in their religious worlds to help.

But there is hope. If I, a nobody from Nigeria, can be counted among this world's most powerful, what would happen if the whole church shifted and began transforming society as we are doing in Ukraine? What if someday we invited world leaders to our global summit and they were compelled to come because Christians were on the leading edge of solving problems? What a day that will be!

WANTED PEOPLE

Whether or not you realize it, you are a wanted person. The world is waiting for you to find your promised land and deliver people from the kingdom of darkness. We all have our own promised lands, commissioned to us from God, those special areas in society that desperately need our help. The world is waiting for the rulers of those promised lands to appear—you and me. Lost people want God's polished arrows to strike at the heart of injustice and unrighteousness. People know they need solutions to their problems and crises. They need to be unshackled. The Bible says:

> For the earnest expectation of the creation eagerly waits for the revealing of the sons of God. For the creation was subjected to futility, not willingly, but because of Him who subjected it in hope; because the creation itself also will be delivered from the bondage of corruption into the glorious liberty of the children of God. For we know that the whole creation groans and labors with birth pangs together until now.
>
> —Romans 8:19–22, NKJV

God has allowed the world to be subjected to futility so that we might set people free with news of His kingdom. We have all the answers. We are indispensable to the health and well-being of our nations. The world simply cannot do without us.

But many Christians don't realize how badly people who don't know Christ are suffering. People in the world face diseases, loneliness, poverty, curses, depression, and more. One person is hooked on alcohol and narcotics; another is suffering from an inability to understand his talent, and so he feels rejected and depressed. Many people are literally tormented inside from sickness, poverty, corruption, addiction, or injustice. The whole world is under the bondage of sin and the slavery of vanity. Who makes man a slave? The devil, who is the prince of this world. Perhaps you have forgotten what it feels like to live without hope. It is like living in hell. Billions of people live that way every day.

I have heard Christians say they cannot preach salvation to some people because they don't have problems. This is never true.

Everyone who does not know Christ, no matter his position in society or his achievements, is suffering from futility. Everyone living without God is in torment. People are waiting for you and me to unlock their chains. They want deliverance from suffering more than they want anything else. Only we, whom God calls kings and judges of the earth, can deliver people from darkness. The key to their salvation is in our hands. Everything the devil does for evil, God can turn into good. His will is that the earth "also will be delivered from the bondage of corruption into the glorious liberty of the children of God" (Rom. 8:21, NKJV). The world is waiting for you!

BLIND LEADING THE BLIND

Until you arrive in your promised land, people will grope around looking for solutions in the wrong places. Some people see the reason for their suffering in economic crisis, high prices, or an unfulfilling career or relationship. The thoughts of such people are concentrated on money, success, and self-gratification. Others think they will be released from suffering by finding a mate, or a new hobby, or prestige. But true happiness and joy are not guaranteed by any of these things. People who live according to the world's standards are confused, and they get into all kinds of trouble and destruction by chasing the wrong answers.

Acts 17:26–27 says God put in nations the desire to seek after Him. Jesus is even called "the desired of all nations" (Hag. 2:7). All people have an inner emptiness that drives them to seek Him. That's why there is so much idol worship in many nations. In a vacuum, people look for something to worship. Some nations worship money, sex, power, sports, and so on. They are waiting for someone to lead them into their proper destinies.

Governments can't set people free from oppression, pain, disappointment, and depression. Only God can give self-esteem when people have none. The government can pass bills, but only the Great Healer can mend a broken soul. We are God's messengers to this generation, called by God to save mankind with the message of the kingdom. The whole world is waiting for you as it groans and travails. It's not enough for our churches to experience revival. Our nations must be transformed. The children of God must show the way of salvation to everyone else.

In the times of ancient Israel, the Spirit of God was upon select people: judges, priests, kings, and prophets. But now God is raising up every believer in the family of God. He grants us all the authority and power of a king and a priest. There is not one Moses, but many.

GIVE YOUR LIFE

Don't be afraid to suffer loss for the sake of Christ. He has already given His life for you. He died to save you. Therefore let us do our utmost that the gospel may be spread throughout the whole world. Jesus said, "For whoever wants to save his life will lose it, but whoever loses his life for me will find it" (Matt. 16:25). This is a choice each of us must make.

When I graduated from university with distinction, I was told that I had a brilliant future. I had a chance to become a member of the Journalists Union in Switzerland and to make a lot of money. But God said to me, "I want you to stay in the Soviet Union and to spread the gospel of Jesus Christ. Will you be a missionary?" It was hard for me to make the decision. I prayed and cried, but in the end I decided to stay in the Soviet Union and follow God's will. Some time later God asked me if I would be willing to give my life for Ukraine. For two whole nights I was not able to sleep because I was thinking about this question. Then suddenly I understood that my life was not my own. The fear of death disappeared and I said, "Yes, Lord, I will give my life for You."

Since that day, my life has only gotten better. God has given me a wonderful calling, a wife and children, and a church that is like family to me. When you give your life for the gospel's sake, you often get back a much better life.

BE A DONKEY

As you shift to occupy your promised land, become a donkey for Christ. This is biblical, as the Gospels say:

> Now when they drew near Jerusalem, and came to Beth-phage, at the Mount of Olives, then Jesus sent two disciples, saying to them, "Go into the village opposite you, and immediately you will find a donkey tied, and a colt with her. Loose them and bring them to Me. And if anyone says anything to you, you shall say, 'The Lord has need of them,' and immediately he will send them."
>
> All this was done that it might be fulfilled which was spoken by the prophet, saying: "Tell the daughter of Zion, 'Behold, your King is coming to you, lowly, and sitting on a donkey, a colt, the foal of a donkey.'"

> So the disciples went and did as Jesus commanded
> them. They brought the donkey and the colt, laid their
> clothes on them, and set Him on them.
>
> —Matthew 21:1–7, NKJV

Jesus needed a donkey and a colt to enter Jerusalem. He needs the same thing to enter your areas of influence. God is saying to us today: "I want to enter your city. I want to enter your school. I want to come into your workplace and your social sphere. I want to be with your family. The harvest is great, and I need laborers and co-workers. I am ready to impact your areas of influence through you. But I need your help. I need someone to carry my influence there."

Anything I have attained in Ukraine or elsewhere is because I have made myself a donkey for Christ. When Jesus entered the city, people welcomed Him with enthusiasm, strewing the road with their garments and with branches from the trees. But I'm sure they barely noticed the animal He rode in on. Yes, this creature had an important mission, to carry the Master. But his mission was about Jesus, not about his own reputation as a worthy pack animal. Carrying the Son of God was enough for him.

That's the example I follow, abasing myself and remembering that people do not need or care about Sunday Adelaja, just as they do not need or care about you. Rather, they need the God you carry. God wants to use us so that His glory might fill the earth. But it is His glory we carry, not our own. Our job is to step surely and confidently, doing our best as that donkey did the day it carried Jesus.

I continue to do my best to make an impact for Christ.

Recently I spoke to the Israeli Parliament. I have met with other countries as well to advise their governments and leaders. I spoke at the United Nations. It's an amazing privilege, but through it all I am reminded that I am God's foolishness—a boy from a Nigerian village that is so small it does not appear on any map. But God has used me to bring a message of personal and national transformation to the world. I hope you will allow your church to shift. I hope you will embrace your calling, find your promised land, and impact your world.

KINGDOM PRINCIPLES
FROM CHAPTER 13

---

1. The Christian community is largely mute on the major issues of the day. The world is waiting for you to find your promised land and deliver people from the kingdom of darkness.

2. Lost people want God's polished arrows to strike at the heart of injustice and unrighteousness. We are indispensable to the health and well-being of our nations.

3. Everyone living without God is in torment

4. Until you arrive in your promised land, people will grope around looking for solutions in the wrong places.

5. The government can pass bills, but only the Great Healer can mend a broken soul.

6. When you give your life for the gospel's sake, you often get back a much better life.

7. God wants to use us so that His glory might fill the earth. It is His glory we carry, not our own.

Epilogue

FROM THE MOMENT I WAS SAVED THE LORD MADE my life to be an example of what a Christian can accomplish when he goes for the best in God. I believe the Lord intends to do the same in every life. We must shift our thinking to allow Him to do so.

In the conclusion of this book I think it will be a benefit and a blessing to share a brief analysis of my personal life. Saved at nineteen years of age, I attended a gospel church (where the Word was preached) for only six months before I left the shores of my country for the atheistic stronghold of Russia. However, I had read so much Bible and Christian literature that my friends thought that I was preparing for a serious university examination, while the more serious believers thought that I was an ordained minister and at least a ten-year-old believer.

I began pursuing God and totally committed to stop any of my previous entangling sin. Before my salvation I had numerous girlfriends, dating freely with them. Once I knew God had forgiven me for the sin of fornication, I vowed never to touch a woman again until I married. It never happened until age twenty-seven, when I met my darling wife, Bose. That is how I discovered the power of holiness and the role of decision in it. Not dating between the ages of nineteen and twenty-seven made people think that I was fanatical. That consecrated lifestyle made me focus on discovering God. The result? Divine encounters and revelations in the school of the Holy Ghost! So much that everywhere I preach or speak now, almost everybody asks me what Bible school or seminary I completed. In the real sense I never completed any. In fact, I was never officially a church member. I will normally tell them I was trained in the wilderness of life. Maximum and absolute pursuit of God produces maximum and absolute discovery of God. If our faith is not absolute it is paralytic. It is either 100 percent faith and commitment or nothing at all.

Even though there was no church, pastor, or fellowship of believers in my years behind the iron curtain, my maximum aspiration for God yielded its undeniable result when communism came down. At the age of thirty-three I had built the largest church in the former Soviet Union. At thirty-five, I built the largest evangelical and charismatic church in Europe. I am happily married and have written over fifty books. Now that I am forty years old, I feel I have maximized my life so much in God that I feel like the apostle Paul, who says he was ready to go be with the Lord but had to be here on Earth because it was better for his followers. I feel I have done so much at forty that I can now dedicate the rest of my life to sharing my experience with the rest of the body of Christ. I feel that every single Christian can be a world changer, a Moses, and a deliverer in his generation. That is how I have taught my members in Kyiv. We have been able to plant over six hundred churches in over forty countries just in the last ten years of ministry.

My friend and spiritual mentor T. L. Osborn once said, "Pastor Sunday is a young old man: young because of his age of less than forty years old, old because at such a young age he has known what old men like me know and has been able to accomplish what many old men like me have not been able to do."

May your life and your church shift for the kingdom of God in Jesus's name! Be blessed!

Notes

CHAPTER 4
BECOMING KINGDOM MINDED

1. Pastors and Ministry Leaders of Sonoma County, CA (facilitated by Pastors' Prayer and Ministry Alliance of Sonoma County), "Pastors in Repentance," http://www .godembassy.org/ru/news/news_publ.php?showdetail=1314 (accessed April 26, 2007).

CHAPTER 8
LEARN TO FIGHT!

1. Alan Cullison, "Man With a Mission: A Nigerian Minister Sets Out to Save Kiev," *Wall Street Journal*, July 21, 2006.

THE WORKBOOK/STUDY GUIDE FOR CHURCH*SHIFT* IS HERE!

The **CHURCHSHIFT** manual is a product of the burden in my heart to maximize resources in the local church. The local church is the biggest and most powerful organization and structure in the world, if we would only learn how to maximize our potential!

Millions of church members in our pews could be taught and equipped to finish the Great Commission quickly, if adequately mobilized. I have come to America to join hands with pastors, help people find their Promised Lands, and encourage them to pursue their callings of God. As a result, the pastors and the local church members they raise up will work in perfect harmony.

Make sure you get the corresponding workbook for this book!

Order today at www.Churchshift.org

This workbook helps local churches affect society and take back their cities and nation for God.

BUILD MEN. BUILD CHURCHES.

Learn from one of the great leaders that inspired Pastor Sunday Adelaja to transform a nation. You can gain wisdom and knowledge from the "father of the Christian men's movement" at: **www.EdCole.org**

"Edwin Louis Cole brought a revolution to our world before I led the revolution. And, thank God, he emptied himself into us through his books. I would like to encourage you to get behind this ministry!" -- PASTOR SUNDAY ADELAJA

ChurchShift
The Movement

"When we are Kingdom-addicted and Kingdom-focused on Kingdom principles, the pastors empower, educate and encourage church members, and the church members take the Kingdom of God into the society."
– SUNDAY ADELAJA

Join the CHURCH*SHIFT* movement!

TEN BENEFITS OF CHURCH*SHIFT!*

1. **CHURCH***SHIFT* will help transform nations by introducing a new way to do church.
2. **CHURCH***SHIFT* reveals how to "pastor without tears."
3. **CHURCH***SHIFT* helps avoid splits and division.
4. **CHURCH***SHIFT* changes our view of our ministry.
5. **CHURCH***SHIFT* inspires us to believe for supernatural outcomes.
6. **CHURCH***SHIFT* equips church members to impact the seven spheres of society.
7. **CHURCH***SHIFT* teaches Kingdom values for societal transformation.
8. **CHURCH***SHIFT* activates the potential of the local church.
9. **CHURCH***SHIFT* helps change nations by emerging from four walls of a church building.
10. **CHURCH***SHIFT* provides the keys for NATIONAL TRANSFORMATION!

CHURCH*SHIFT* Leadership Summits are coming to your area! Watch for details on:

www.CHURCHSHIFT.org

Sunday Adelaja and the ministry of CHURCH*SHIFT* are privileged to be leaders in the SECOND BILLION movement worldwide.

The Internet will gain the next billion users within a few years. Proctor and Gamble is adding a billion customers in just three years. A billion new cell phones will be sold this year. Coca Cola sells a billion Cokes every day. With one billion Christians in the world today, our goal is to double and win the Second Billion in a decade.

The Second Billion movement is networking the billion Christians in the world today with the best methods and means to work together to plant five million new churches and win another billion people to Christ. CHURCH*SHIFT* brings to the Second Billion movement:

1. The value and ability to raise "deliverers" not just members
2. Training to release people to their field in society
3. Refocusing 80% of church activity to bring the Kingdom into society and take back the culture.
4. Raising the standard of "ministry" to include societal transformation.
5. Training for members to impose Kingdom values on the seven spheres of influence.

Join the Second Billion movement today! www.BILLION.tv

HISTORY MAKERS BIBLE SCHOOL

ONE LIFE CHANGING WEEKEND A MONTH
WITH PASTOR SUNDAY ADELAJA

from September *to* May

CONTACT INFO:
267.266.0236
267.265.5491
e-mail:dean@hmbs.org
www.hmbs.org

The Founder and President of the
School Pastor Sunday Adelaja
an honorary Doctor of Humanity
(U.N.O.). Journalist, International
Speaker, Advisor to Heads of
States, Advocate of National
Transformation.

*"For Those Who Want to
Change Their World for Christ."*

pastorsunday.org
godembassy.org